Sport Fish of the Pacific

FS Books:
Sport Fish of Florida
Sport Fish of the Gulf of Mexico
Sport Fish of the Atlantic
Sport Fish of Fresh Water
Sport Fish of the Pacific

Baits, Rigs & Tackle
Sportsman's Best: Sailfish
Sportsman's Best: Inshore Fishing
Sportsman's Best: Snapper & Grouper
Sportsman's Best: Offshore
Annual Fishing Planner
The Angler's Cookbook

Florida Sportsman Magazine
Shallow Water Angler Magazine
Florida Sportsman Fishing Charts
Lawsticks
Law Boatstickers

Edited by Eric Wickstrom
Art Direction by Drew Wickstrom and Jim Henderson
Copy Edited by Jerry McBride

First Edition
Second Printing
Copyright 2004 by Florida Sportsman
Printed in the United States of America
ISBN 0-936240-28-8

Sport Fish of the Pacific

By Vic Dunaway

Original Illustrations by

Kevin R. Brant

Joe Suroviec

www.floridasportsman.com

CONTENTS

Preface   7

Illustration: The Pacific   8

Introduction: The Pacific Coast   9

Introduction: How to Use this Book   10

Chapter 1
Mackerels and Tunas   14
Albacore, Bigeye Tuna, Black Skipjack, Bullet
Mackerel, Frigate Mackerel, Gulf Sierra, Pacific
Bonito, Pacific Mackerel, Sierra, Skipjack Tuna,
Southern Bluefin, Tuna, Striped Bonito, Wahoo,
Yellowfin Tuna

Chapter 2
The Billfishes   30
Black Marlin, Blue Marlin, Sailfish, Shortbill
Spearfish, Striped Marlin, Swordfish

Chapter 3
The Jacks   38
African Pompano, Almaco Jack, Bigeye Trevally,
Bigeye Scad, Black Jack, Bluefin Trevally,
Gafftopsail Pompano, Golden Jack, Green Jack,
Jack Mackerel, Leatherjack, Mexican Scad,
Pacific Crevalle Jack, Pacific Lookdown, Pacific
Permit, Paloma Pompano, Pilotfish, Rainbow,
Runner, Roosterfish, Threadfin Jack, Ulua,
Yellowtail

Chapter 4
Rugged Individuals   62
California Sheepshead, Dolphin, Great
Barracuda, Green Sturgeon, Pacific Barracuda,
Pacific, Bonefish, Pacific Ladyfish, Tarpon,
Tripletail, White Sturgeon

Chapter 5
The Croakers   74
Bairdiella, Black Croaker, California Corbina,
Gulf Corvina, Highfin Kingcroaker,
Orangemouth Corvina, Pacific Drum, Pacific
Kingcroaker, Queenfish, Shortfin Corvina,
Spotfin Croaker, Stolzmann's Corvina, Striped
Corvina, Totuava, White Corvina, White
Croaker, White Seabass, Yellowfin Croaker

Chapter 6
The Flatfishes   94
Bigmouth Sole, California Halibut, Pacific
Sanddab, Butter Sole, C-O Sole, Diamond
Turbot, Flathead Sole, Pacific Halibut, Petrale
Sole, Rock Sole, Sand Sole, Starry Flounder

Chapter 7
Salmons, Chars and "Trouts"   108
Arctic Char, Chinook Salmon, Chum Salmon,
Coho Salmon, Cutthroat Trout, Dolly Varden,
Pink Salmon, Sockeye Salmon, Steelhead

Chapter 8
The Surfperches   118
Barred Surfperch, Black Perch, Calico
Surfperch, Rainbow Surfperch, Redtail
Surfperch, Rubberlip Seaperch, Shiner Perch,
Silver Surfperch, Striped Surfperch, Walleye
Surfperch, White Seaperch

Chapter 9
The Rockfishes   130
Black-and-Yellow Rockfish, Black Rockfish, Blue
Rockfish, Bocaccio, Brown Rockfish, California
Scorpionfish, Canary Rockfish, Chilipepper,
China Rockfish, Copper Rockfish, Cowcod,
Grass Rockfish, Greenspotted Rockfish, Kelp
Rockfish, Olive Rockfish, Quillback Rockfish,
Redbanded Rockfish, Redstripe Rockfish, Rosy
Rockfish, Silvergray Rockfish, Speckled
Rockfish, Tiger Rockfish, Vermilion Rockfish,
Widow Rockfish, Yelloweye Rockfish,
Yellowtail Rockfish

Chapter 10
Cods and Kin   146
Pacific Cod, Pacific Hake, Pacific Tomcod,
Walleye Pollock

Chapter 11
Lingcod and Greenlings   152
Kelp Greenling, Lingcod, Rock Greenling,
Whitespotted Greenling

Chapter 12
The Sculpins 158
Cabezon, Pacific Staghorn Sculpin, Red Irish
Lord, Yellow Irish Lord

Chapter 13
Basses and Groupers 164
Barred Sand Bass, Black Sea Bass, Broomtail
Grouper, Flag Cabrilla, Giant Hawkfish,
Goldspotted Sand Bass, Goliath Grouper, Gulf
Coney, Gulf Grouper, Kelp Bass, Leopard
Grouper, Panama Graysby, Sawtail Grouper,
Snowy Grouper, Spotted Cabrilla, Spotted Sand
Bass, Starstudded Grouper, Striped Bass

Chapter 14
The Snappers 184
Amarillo Snapper, Barred Pargo, Blue-and-Gold
Snapper, Colorado Snapper, Jordan's Snapper,
Mullet Snapper, Pacific Cubera Snapper, Pacific
Red Snapper, Spotted Rose Snapper

Chapter 15
The Snooks 194
Black Snook, White Snook, Little Snook,
Longspine Snook, Bigeye Snook,
Humpback Snook

Chapter 16
The Sharks 200
Angel Shark, Blacktip Shark, Blue Shark,
Bonnethead, Bull Shark, Common Thresher,
Dusky Shark, Galapagos Shark, Gray
Smoothhound, Great Hammerhead, Lemon
Shark, Leopard Shark, Nurse Shark, Oceanic
Whitetip Shark, Pacific Sharpnose Shark,
Salmon Shark, Scalloped Hammerhead,
Shortfin Mako, Silky Shark, Smooth
Hammerhead, Soupfin Shark, Spiny Dogfish,
Tiger Shark, White Shark, Whitenose Shark

Chapter 17
Rays and Relatives 224
Big Skate, California Skate, Shovelnose
Guitarfish, Pacific Electric Ray, Round Stingray,
Largetooth Sawfish

Chapter 18
The Grunts 230
Blackbar Grunt, Brassy Grunt, Burrito Grunt,
Latin Grunt, Mojarra Grunt, Pacific Grunt,
Pacific Porkfish, Salema, Sargo, Spottail Grunt,
Wavyline Grunt

Chapter 19
A Miscellany 238
Pacific Porgy, Ocean Whitefish, Opaleye, Pacific
Spadefish, California Moray, California
Lizardfish, Bullseye Puffer, Mojarra, Azure
Parrotfish, Finescale Triggerfish, Cutlassfish, King
Angelfish, Chihuil, Long-Barbled Catfish, Pacific
Needlefish, Barred Needlefish, Sharksucker,
Remora, White Mullet, Striped Mullet,
Hawaiian Bigeye, Yellow Bobo

Chapter 20
Herrings and Baitfishes 252
American Shad, California Grunion, California
Killifish, Capelin, Deepbody Anchovy, Eulachon,
Jacksmelt, Longfin Halfbeak, Longfin Smelt,
Northern Anchovy, Pacific Herring, Pacific Sand
Lance, Pacific Sardine, Pacific Saury, Rainbow
Smelt, Round Herring, Surf Smelt, Thread
Herring, Threadfin Shad, Whitebait Smelt

Index 264

About the author 272

Preface

Knowing Your Pacific Fish

If you fish in that great Pacific bowl teeming with hundreds of different species, this is the book you must have.

Here, for the first time, is a complete guidebook to all the fish, providing you details for identification, food value, ways to catch them, usual sizes and world records and ranges.

Every entry features an original color illustration meticulously done exclusively for Sport Fish of the Pacific.

Both common and Latin names are given, so there can be no mistake about that critter on the end of your line. But simplicity and ease of use for the typical angler are the key goals in presenting this latest entry in our fast-selling Sport Fish series.

Why not just use the Atlantic book?

Why not just call a zebra a horse?

The Pacific is very different, all because of a little strip of land called the Isthmus of Panama that fully developed only three million years ago. The risen connector between North and South America forever changed the currents, temperatures and salinities of each ocean.

More importantly for the fisherman, the volcanic eruptions forming the Isthmus reorganized the biodiversity of life in the seas. Evolution moved quickly, in geologic terms, that is.

Most species that had roamed the pre-Isthmus sea evolved into different-looking characters, fitting the same basic niches in the astonishingly varied tableau of marine life. A few remained unchanged, as you'll see.

At any rate, Sport Fish of the Pacific is dedicated to you, the angler, whether you're sorting out the sometimes confusing salmons or the always alluring snook.

—Karl Wickstrom

Publisher

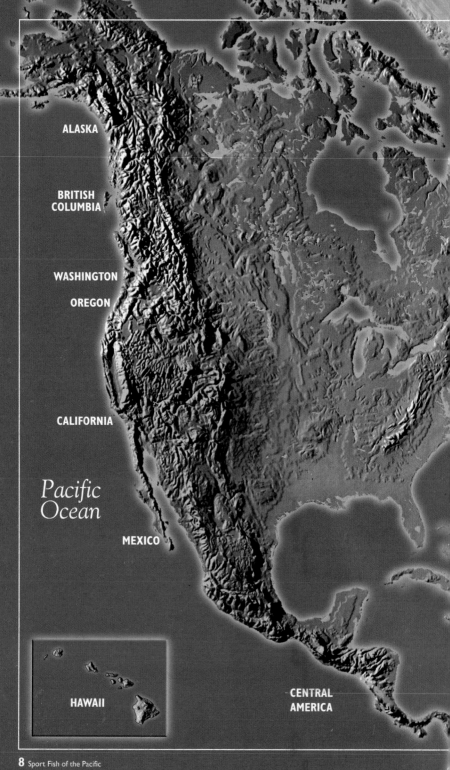

ALASKA

BRITISH
COLUMBIA

WASHINGTON

OREGON

CALIFORNIA

*Pacific
Ocean*

MEXICO

HAWAII

CENTRAL
AMERICA

INTRODUCTION

This is a book designed solely for the fisherman, and it fills a glaring gap. Other reference works are available, true, but all of them fall into one of two categories:

(1) Instructional books on angling that deal with a comparatively few prominent gamefish but do little to alleviate the fisherman's need for knowledge about the many lesser species he is sure to encounter, or

(2) Scientific guides that blanket everything with gills, making it a considerable challenge for the angler to track down an unknown catch from among a seemingly endless assortment of tiny or obscure species that are of interest only to biologists and serious students.

So the aim here is to provide the sportsman not only with accurate color illustrations and basic information about the many great sport species that swim Pacific waters from the frigid climes of Alaska to the balmy trop-

ics of Central America, but also to do the same for just about any other fish he might find, whether it be a welcome catch or an unwanted interloper. In all, more than 250 species are encompassed in these pages, ranging from the most prestigious kinds down to tiny baitfishes that so many anglers depend upon to produce catche's of bigger game. And everything in between.

Large and small, inshore and offshore, beautiful and ugly, desirable and detestable, all are part of the angler's experience.

Over and above its value as an identification guide, the book provides the basic information that is so necessary to angling success—the range of each species, the habitat in which it is most likely to be hooked, the best kind of tackle and bait to use, and even its table qualities. No other book contains such critical core information for so many different kinds of Pacific Coast fishes.

HOW TO USE
THE BOOK

It would be great if all the fish could be conveniently grouped according to where the angler goes to catch them. If that were the case then the surf fisherman, say, could find his potential line-up of catches in one chapter, while the bay angler and big-game troller and party boat fisherman could look for theirs in others. Unfortunately, such a neat arrangement cannot work, simply because too many fish wander over too many different types and depths of water. For instance, on the same day when some anglers are catching Rockfish in coastal backwaters, others might well be taking them from the surf, and still others hauling them in on a party boat far offshore. In like manner, many pelagic gamefish are not unusual catches close to the beach, or even from piers.

The book is arranged, therefore, so that most of the chapters cover a single family of fishes, which makes for handy identification because family members generally exhibit physical similarities, even though they differ in size and color. A few prominent species, however, are not members of large families, and these have been bunched into a chapter called Rugged Individuals. Others, such as Baitfishes, have been laid out in arbitrary groupings according to similarity of habitat or habit, or according to the way they are viewed by the majority of anglers. Regardless, the illustrations and the careful indexing will make it easy for the fisherman to find any of them for quick reference.

THE INDIVIDUAL LISTINGS

Heading the entry for each species is its most widely used common name, with the scientific name just below it. Although every effort has been made to keep the book non-technical, the inclusion of the scientific name is necessary for positive identification, because common names can vary from area to area, or even in the same area. The other covered categories are as follows:

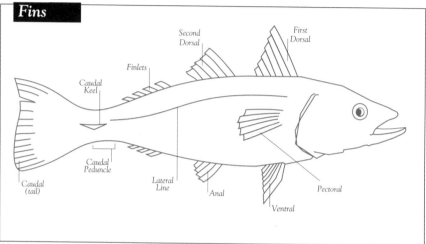

Here's a typical configuration of fins useful for identification.

DESCRIPTION: Just as common names often vary, so does coloration in many fish. The written description, therefore, is necessary to point out identifying features that, in combination with the drawing, should serve to make for accurate identification.

SIZE: The usual size spread of the fish taken by sportsmen is noted here, along with an estimate as to the potential maximum size as well.

RANGE: This paragraph gives the usual distribution of the subject species along the Pacific Coast from Alaska through Panama only—not its entire range, which for many species is far wider, perhaps even circling the globe. Also, the reader should be aware that certain fish are capable of wandering far beyond the territory where they are staple catches. The odds, however, are heavily stacked against the possibility of catching those fish at extreme ends of their range.

WHERE TO FISH: Obviously, finding a productive fishing area generally requires trial-and-error, study and whatever advice can be gleaned from local anglers. Although this paragraph can't tell you exactly where to toss your bait, it will provide a good starting point for your personal search by disclosing such important clues as preferred bottom type or habitat and most productive depths.

FOOD VALUE: Nearly all fish are edible and nutritious but some are not very appetizing for one reason or another. Maybe they're too bony or the flesh too red to suit personal taste. And taste, of course, is highly subjective. The author has attempted to balance his own opinion with those expressed by other anglers and seafood consumers. If you don't agree with the stated assessment, fine. At least you won't have to worry, because the only species that should be avoided because of possible toxicity are the puffers. In Hawaii and some other tropical areas of the world, a poison called ciguatera is sometimes found in large specimens of many kinds of predatory fish, but it has never been a problem in the tropical eastern Pacific.

GAME QUALITIES: Again, this opinion is based on the author's personal experience plus many years of conversation with anglers and sportfishing professionals. Though not as variable as taste, fighting attributes of various fish species are also subject to some debate. Much depends on the tackle used, and also on the angler's own experience in handling the tackle and playing fish.

TACKLE: Broad tips are given here as to the most suitable types of tackle, and perhaps other angling advice.

BAITS AND LURES: These are the natural and artificial baits that have been proven effective by many anglers. With dead baits and cut baits, the range of choices is always very wide. Even those species that seem to prefer baits of shellfish origin will often accept baits from finfish. In many cases, of course live baits produce far more strikes than dead baits, and that fact is noted where appropriate. And any fish that will take live bait will also take artificial lures that are chosen according to past experience, and presented and retrieved in appealing fashion.

FISHERY LAWS AND MANAGEMENT

Every angler has both the moral and legal obligation to help preserve fish stocks and habitat. Nowadays he faces—even in one jurisdiction—a sometimes complex and bewildering array of regulations that cover licensing, size limits, bag limits, closed seasons—perhaps even staggered seasons for the same fish in different locations. Now, multiply that by all the states and provinces covered in this work and the futility of trying to include all the regulations here should be obvious.

Of one thing, there is no doubt. The angler will need a different license, or set of permits as the case may be, for every different jurisdiction in which he plans to fish. This is true not only of the U.S. and Canada, but also of Mexico and Central American countries as well. Information concerning license needs and regulations affecting targeted species is widely available from guides, boat captains, marinas, bait and tackle stores and resorts along the entire coast. You can also contact state and provincial fish management agencies at the following addresses:

UNITED STATES
Alaska Dept. of Fish and Game
P.O. Box 25526
Juneau, AK 99802-5526
(907) 465-4100

Washington Dept. of Fish and Wildlife
600 Capitol Way North
Olympia, WA 98501-1091
(360) 902-2700

Oregon Dept. of Fish and Wildlife
P.O. Box 59
Portland, OR 97207
(503) 872-5252

California Dept. of Fish and Game
Fisheries Program Branch
1416 9th St.
Sacramento, CA 95814
(916) 653-7664

BRITISH COLUMBIA
Ministry of Water, Air and Land Protection
P.O. Box 9339 Stn. Prov. Govt.
Victoria, BC
V8W9M1
(250) 387-1161

The widely diverse Mackerel family, which includes Tunas and Bonitos, might well provide more sport for more saltwater anglers than any other group of fishes. Its members range in size from little Tinker Mackerel that delight spinning and fly casting enthusiasts, to the great Bluefin and Yellowfin Tunas that rank right alongside Marlin and Sailfish in the esteem of big-game fishermen. And in between there is a lineup of middleweight and lightweight gamesters with the strength and speed to test every kind of sporting tackle. These include the speedy Albacore and various smaller Tunas and Bonitos, plus some pretty hefty species on the Mackerel side of the family, including the Wahoo and Sierra. As a group, these fishes are all wanderers, some migrating close to shore with changing seasons and water temperatures, others roaming the high seas following currents and food supply—all of which means that one or more of them is at least seasonally available to onshore and near-shore fishermen, as well as to those who travel far from land on charter, party and private boats. The fact that nearly all the Mackerels and Tunas make fine eating is a mixed blessing. Many species are commercially valuable, long over-exploited, and heavily regulated.

Mackerels and Tunas

Albacore

Bigeye Tuna

Black Skipjack

Bullet Mackerel

Frigate Mackerel

Gulf Sierra

Pacific Bonito

Pacific Mackerel

Sierra

Skipjack Tuna

Southern Bluefin Tuna

Striped Bonito

Wahoo

Yellowfin Tuna

Albacore

Thunnus alalunga

OTHER NAMES:

Atun Blanco
Tombo
Ahipalaha

RANGE: *British Columbia to southern California; found mostly in temperate waters, straying occasionally to subtropical areas.*

WHERE TO FISH: *The open sea. Schools (often mixed with Skipjack Tuna and/or Yellowfin Tuna) can be found by blind trolling or by roaming and searching for surface activity*

DESCRIPTION: Body is dark blue above and silvery below. Dorsal and anal fins are yellow. Its most obvious feature is the long pectoral fin with pointed tip that extends all the way past both dorsal fins. Small Bigeye Tuna also have long pectorals but the tips are rounded.

SIZE: Common at 10-20 pounds; occasionally tops 40 pounds and, very rarely, reaches about 80 pounds. World record 88 pounds, 2 ounces.

FOOD VALUE: Its white meat is commercially the most valuable of the Tuna clan but actually it is very bland and less tasty than the flesh of Yellowfin or Bluefin.

GAME QUALITIES: It's a Tuna; so pound-for-pound it ranks among the best battlers.

TACKLE: Any type of ocean gear with lines up to 50-pound test is effectively used for trolling. However for tossing out live baits, fairly long rods are better, fitted with reels designed for smooth casting and spooled with 20- or 30-pound test line.

LURES AND BAITS: Various lures and rigged baits are effective for trollers, but the best Albacore action comes after schools are found. Then anglers aboard charter, party or private boats generally drift while chumming with live Anchovies and baiting with the same. When "hot" the fish will also take dead fish and squid, and also artificial lures, primarily metallic squids. All too often, though, you'll need not only live bait but also light leader and a long cast to coax much action.

Bigeye Tuna

Thunnus obesus

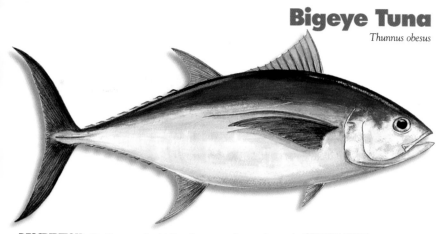

DESCRIPTION: Similar to the Yellowfin at a glance, but the gold stripe common to the Yellowfin is replaced by a stripe of iridescent blue on the live fish. The first dorsal fin is deep yellow, the second dorsal and anal fins are light yellow, and the finlets are bright yellow edged with black. The eye is indeed larger than that of other Tunas, but this might not be readily apparent without a side-by-side comparison.

SIZE: Runs to about the same sizes as the Yellowfin Tuna—from a few pounds to more than 400 pounds. World record 435 pounds.

FOOD VALUE: Excellent.

GAME QUALITIES: Among the strongest and most rugged of fighters.

TACKLE: Seldom targeted, it is usually caught while chumming for Yellowfins or other Tunas, or by deep drifting. Tackle choices would be the same as for Yellowfin Tuna.

LURES AND BAITS: Live baitfish, squid, and large rigged dead baits have all been used with success. Small surfacing fish will take trolled feathers and spoons.

OTHER NAMES:

Ahi po'o nui
Ahi

RANGE: California to Panama; straggles northward; also Hawaii.

WHERE TO FISH: The open sea. As the big eye indicates, the big ones stay deep most of the time and so may not be as rare as the low number of angling encounters would seem to indicate. Small, schooling fish will feed at or near the surface, sometimes mixing with other Tunas.

Black Skipjack

Euthynnus lineatus

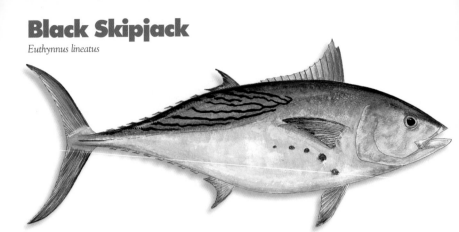

OTHER NAMES:

Spotted Tuna
Mackerel Tuna
Mexican
Little Tunny

RANGE: *California to Panama; rarely Hawaii.*

WHERE TO FISH: *Usually found mixing with schools of Skipjack and Yellowfin Tuna, feeding at the surface.*

DESCRIPTION: It is quickly distinguishable from the Skipjack Tuna by the stripes, which are on the upper sides instead of the lower sides and belly. The back is dark blue.

SIZE: Averages 2-6 pounds, but is not uncommon at 10 pounds or more, and can reach perhaps 30 pounds.

FOOD VALUE: Good.

GAME QUALITIES: Excellent fighter, pound for pound.

TACKLE: Very light spinning, casting or trolling tackle would be ideal, but heavy tackle is often used because of the possibility of larger Tunas in the same area.

LURES AND BAITS: Many lures will work, but bucktail jigs, metallic jigs and spoons probably will get the most strikes. Small fish or squid are fine natural baits.

Bullet Mackerel

Auxis rochei

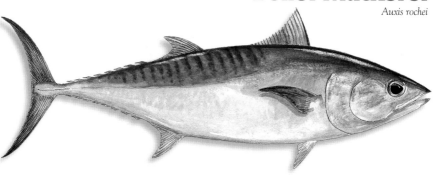

DESCRIPTION: This and the Frigate Mackerel are similar in appearance, range and all other aspects and are thought by some authorities to be the same species. The back is blue or deep purple to almost black Lower sides are white. A scaleless area above the lateral line contains about 15 dark bars that are slightly oblique, nearly vertical.

SIZE: Usually under a pound; may grow to about 4 pounds. World record 3 pounds, 8 ounces.

FOOD VALUE: Poor by most tastes; dark and oily.

GAME QUALITIES: A good fighter for its size.

TACKLE: Light spinning.

LURES AND BAITS: Often trolled for, or cast for, as bait for larger fish, using small spoons or jigs. A ready biter on minnows or most any small natural bait, live or dead.

RANGE: *California to Panama; sometimes farther north.*

WHERE TO FISH: *The open sea, but often swings close to shore.*

Frigate Mackerel

Auxis thazard

OTHER NAMES:

Boo Hoo
Bonito

RANGE: *California to Panama; sometimes farther north.*

WHERE TO FISH: *Mostly the open sea, but often swings close to shore.*

DESCRIPTION: This species looks very much like the Bullet mackerel but the scaleless area on the rear portion of the back is marked with nearly horizontal wavy lines, rather than more vertical bold stripes.

SIZE: Averages a foot; rarely reaches 2 feet.

FOOD VALUE: Poor by most tastes; dark and oily.

GAME QUALITIES: A good fighter for its size.

TACKLE: Light spinning.

LURES AND BAITS: Often trolled for, or cast for, as bait for larger fish, using small spoons or jigs. A ready biter on minnows or other small natural baits, live or dead.

Gulf Sierra

Scomberomorus concolor

DESCRIPTION: Similar in silhouette to the Sierra, but males have no spots at all and females only a few brown spots. Color is dark blue above, silvery below.

SIZE: Averages a couple of pounds; maximum around 8 pounds.

FOOD VALUE: Very good.

GAME QUALITIES: A sporty foe on light tackle.

TACKLE: Spinning, baitcasting and fly outfits can all be used but spinning is best because the faster retrieve of a spinning reel is sometimes needed to move a lure fast enough to attract the speedy fish.

LURES AND BAITS: Best lures are small jigs and silver spoons, but many others work, including topwater plugs at times. Best baits are small silvery baitfish, live shrimp and drifted strips.

OTHER NAMES:

Gulf Mackerel
Monterey
Spanish Mackerel

RANGE: *Now limited to the northern portion of the Gulf of California, Mexico, although once abundant in California as far north as Monterey Bay.*

WHERE TO FISH: *Close inshore.*

Pacific Bonito

Sarda chiliensis

OTHER NAMES:

California Bonito

RANGE: *Alaska to Baja California.*

WHERE TO FISH: *Runs mostly close to shore and is often available to anglers from piers and jetties as well as boats.*

DESCRIPTION: Body is greenish blue above and silvery below; marked by diagonal stripes on upper sides and back.

SIZE: Most run 4-8 pounds but fish of 10-15 pounds are not rare and the maximum is perhaps 25 pounds. World record 21 pounds, 3 ounces.

FOOD VALUE: Good but flesh is dark.

GAME QUALITIES: Excellent fighter and among the strongest, pound for pound.

TACKLE: Livebait outfits with long rods and either spinning or casting reels are dominant, but spinning and smaller baitcasting outfits are fine, as are light classes of ocean trolling gear. With casting tackle, high-speed reels are highly desirable.

LURES AND BAITS: Silvery, schooling baitfishes are best, but squid and shrimp will take fish. For casting or trolling, jigs and spoons are good but often must be cranked at super-fast speed to draw strikes.

Pacific Mackerel

Scomber japonicus

DESCRIPTION: Color is blue or green above, silvery below. Has many diagonal lines on upper sides, but no markings below the lateral line.

SIZE: Averages less than a foot long; occasionally to 15 inches. World record 4 pounds, 12 ounces.

FOOD VALUE: Good but oily; excellent smoked.

GAME QUALITIES: Hard striker and fast runner. Good fight on very light spinning lines.

TACKLE: Light spinning provides the best sport. Heavier tackle is often used, especially when large catches of the fish are sought for food or bait.

LURES AND BAITS: Small minnows, strip baits and shrimp are always good, as are small jigs, spoons and flies.

OTHER NAMES:

**Tinker Mackerel
Escombro Serracho**

RANGE: *Primarily British Columbia to Baja California, Mexico.*

WHERE TO FISH: *Largely coastal but also roams offshore and in large bays.*

Sierra

Scomboromorus sierra

OTHER NAMES:

Sierra Mackerel
Pacific Spanish
Mackerel

RANGE: *Southern California to Panama.*

WHERE TO FISH: *Most are taken close to shore or in bays, and just about anywhere along the Mexican and Central American coast.*

DESCRIPTION: The sides are silvery with numerous round orange spots. The first dorsal fin is black with a white fringe. The second dorsal fin is tinged with yellow and with a black margin. To anglers, it is virtually a dead ringer for the Spanish Mackerel of the Atlantic.

SIZE: Averages a good 3 or 4 pounds with 6- to 8-pounders being very common. Maximum is around 20 pounds.

FOOD VALUE: Very good.

GAME QUALITIES: Terrific fighter on light tackle. Fast strikes and faster runs are their hallmarks.

TACKLE: Light tackle provides great sport with Sierras. Spinning, baitcasting and fly outfits are all widely used but spinning is best because the faster retrieve of a spinning reel is sometimes needed to move a lure fast enough to attract the speedy fish.

LURES AND BAITS: Best lures are small white nylon jigs and silver spoons, but many others, including topwater at times, will draw strikes. Flies should be small with lots of flash. Best baits are small silvery baitfish and drifted strips of fish or squid.

Skipjack Tuna

Katsuwonus pelamis

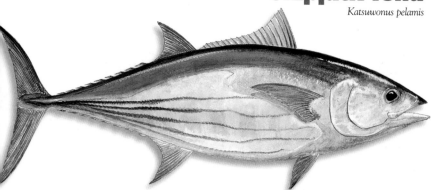

DESCRIPTION: Four to six horizontal stripes on lower half of the body distinguish it from others of its clan. The back is dark purplish blue, lower sides and belly silvery.

SIZE: Runs in schools of similar-size fish, usually 2-6 pounds, but can exceed 15 pounds and sometimes approaches 50. World record 45 pounds, 4 ounces.

FOOD VALUE: The flesh is very dark and not appealing to many, but is very good and nutritious.

GAME QUALITIES: A terrific light-tackle battler.

TACKLE: Large schools are often encountered at the surface and provide fine targets for all sorts of casting outfits, including fly rods. Trollers also have great sport with light classes of trolling tackle and small feathers, spoons and trolling lures.

LURES AND BAITS: For casting, bucktail jigs, metallic jigs and spoons often work, but may have to be scaled closely to the size of the bait on which the fish are feeding. Bucktail flies with flashy Mylar or similar material can also produce. The same lures plus feathers, artificial squids and small offshore trolling lures are good devices for trolling.

OTHER NAMES:

Striped Tuna
Oceanic Bonito
Aku

RANGE: British Columbia to Panama; also Hawaii. Skipjacks are far more common in subtropical and tropical waters than in temperate.

WHERE TO FISH: The deep sea.

Southern Bluefin Tuna

Thunnus maccoyi

OTHER NAMES:

**Pacific Bluefin
Giant Tuna
Black Tuna
Maguro**

RANGE: *Alaska to Baja California, Mexico; rarely in Hawaii. Best fishing is off San Diego and Baja California in the summer.*

WHERE TO FISH: *Usually the deep sea but occasionally sweeps fairly close to shore, especially around offshore islands.*

DESCRIPTION: The Southern Bluefin was long thought to be the same as, or a subspecies of, the Atlantic Bluefin (*T. thynnus*) but it is now classified as a separate species. Color of the chunky body is dark blue above, shading to silver below. The belly and lower sides wear white spots or lines. It is distinguishable from other Tunas of our area by its short pectoral fins, not extending past the first dorsal fin.

SIZE: Schools run roughly in the same sizes, from a few pounds up to about 50 pounds. In the past, 200-pounders were fairly common, but commercial over-fishing riddled the stocks and today 100-pounders are prizes. Longline records indicate the Pacific Bluefin might reach 400 pounds. World record 348 pounds, 5 ounces.

FOOD VALUE: Excellent.

GAME QUALITIES: For its size, the Bluefin is one of the toughest of all fish, displaying strength, stamina and speed.

TACKLE: Ocean trolling and standup tackle should be scaled to the expected size of the fish. Tackle in the 50-pound class is not too heavy for sport, but small school fish are great matchups for 12- to 30-pound lines. Heavy spinning gear is another good tackle choice for the smaller fish.

LURES AND BAITS: Although very selective much of the time, Bluefins are caught on a variety of trolled offerings, such as feathers, plugs and offshore trolling lures. Rigged dead baits are good too. All sizes of Bluefins respond readily to chumming and this is a standard approach. Anglers and crews toss out live baits such as Anchovies or Herring to get the fish interested, and then feed them the same baits on a hook.

Striped Bonito

Sarda orientalis

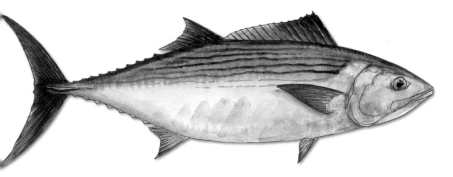

DESCRIPTION: Difficult to distinguish from the Pacific Bonito, but the stripes on its upper sides are more nearly horizontal than diagonal. Shape is also a bit chunkier. The back and upper sides are metallic blue. Sides and belly are silver.

SIZE: Most run 4-8 pounds; can exceed 20 pounds. World record 23 pounds, 8 ounces.

FOOD VALUE: Good but meat is dark.

GAME QUALITIES: Terrific on light line.

TACKLE: Livebait outfits with long rods and either spinning or casting reels are dominant, but spinning and smaller baitcasting outfits are fine, as are light classes of ocean trolling gear. With casting tackle, high-speed reels are highly desirable.

LURES AND BAITS: Silvery, schooling baitfishes are best, but squid and shrimp will take fish. For casting or trolling, jigs and spoons are good but often must be cranked at super-fast speed to draw strikes.

OTHER NAMES:

Mexican Bonito
Oriental Bonito

RANGE: California to Panama; also Hawaii.

WHERE TO FISH: Close to shore, usually near schooling baitfish concentrations and often mixed with other Bonitos and Tunas.

Wahoo

Acanthocybium solandri

OTHER NAMES:

Peto
Ono
Guahu

RANGE: *California to Panama; also Hawaii.*

WHERE TO FISH: *The deep sea, especially around rips, weedlines, upwellings and other favorable feeding locations.*

DESCRIPTION: A long, slender body, vivid zebra-like stripes of white and deep blue or black. and a narrow, elongated mouth equipped with razor-sharp teeth, make a live or freshly caught Wahoo impossible to mistake for any other fish.

SIZE: Most catches run 20-50 pounds, but individuals pushing 100 pounds are not rare, and the potential is to more than 150. World record 158 pounds, 8 ounces.

FOOD VALUE: The flesh is rather dry but is white and mild. Excellent smoked.

GAME QUALITIES: The fight of a Wahoo features speed—speed that barely slows through several dazzling runs. The Wahoo may strike a surface-trolled bait in spectacular, greyhounding fashion, but seldom jumps after being hooked.

TACKLE: Ocean trolling tackle or standup gear with lines testing 30-50 pounds rate as the top choice, but many Wahoo are caught on heavy Marlin outfits and still give a fine account of themselves.

LURES AND BAITS: Deep trolling is much more likely to produce strikes from Wahoo than is surface trolling, although many have been taken on top. A leading lure for trolling is a heavy red or orange feather in combination with a whole small baitfish or strip of fish. Frequent catches are also made by anglers drifting or still-fishing with live baits, or even casting with metallic jigs.

Yellowfin Tuna

Thunnus albacares

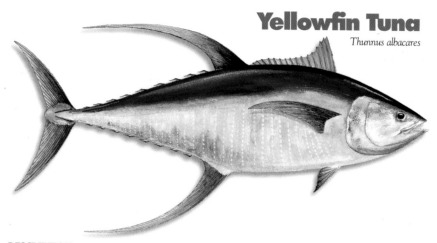

DESCRIPTION: Large fish are easy to identify because their second dorsal and anal fins are very long and lunate. Small Yellowfins, however, lack this trademark and are difficult to distinguish from Bigeye and Bluefin Tunas of similar size. Check the pectoral fins. Those of the Yellowfin extend to a point just below the beginning of the second dorsal. Finlets in back of the dorsal are yellow, trimmed in black. A gold stripe runs along the upper side, and the light underside usually shows grayish wavy or broken lines.

SIZE: Schools of like-size fish may range anywhere from a few pounds to 50 or 100 pounds. Individuals up to 300 pounds are reasonably common, and the maximum is perhaps 400 pounds. World record 388 pounds, 12 ounces.

FOOD VALUE: One of the best.

GAME QUALITIES: Like other Tunas they are about the toughest of all fish on a pound-for-pound basis, and since Yellowfins are commonly caught in much larger sizes than Pacific Bluefins they are a real handful of trouble.

TACKLE: For bigger fish, standup or trolling outfits with lines testing at least 50 pounds, if not 80, are called for. Lighter line classes—20 and 30—can also be used effectively in experienced hands, even for fish over 100 pounds.

LURES AND BAITS: Many Yellowfins are caught trolling with offshore trolling lures or rigged baits, but the best approach is to anchor or slow-drift over a reef or known productive area and bring in the fish by chumming liberally with small baitfish such as Anchovies or Sardines, or even chunks of fish or squid. When responding to such chum Yellowfins will often hit not only the live baits, but also artificial lures such as metallic jigs.

OTHER NAMES:

Allison Tuna
Ahi

RANGE: California to Panama; occasionally farther north; also Hawaii. Best fishing is from Baja California, Mexico, southward, with much effort taking place aboard long-range boats out of San Diego.

WHERE TO FISH: The open sea; frequently found near reef dropoffs, deep, rocky shorelines of islands, upwellings or any situation that concentrates baitfishes. Big ones school with porpoises, thus often giving away their presence to commercial fishermen.

n the world of offshore angling, the great billfishes make up the royal hierarchy. A couple of the big Tunas are equally tough to land but the fish that wear bills stand alone in combining speed and stamina with wild spectacle. They are among the swiftest fish in the sea and all spend a considerable portion of their fighting time in the air. But which one is biggest? Without starting an argument let's call it a tie between the Blue and Black Marlins. In Pacific sportfishing records, the Black stands a bit bigger—1,560 pounds to 1,376—but that's only for catches that meet strict angling standards. Both types are said to have been recorded at well over 2,000 pounds by commercial fishermen, and one Blue caught in Hawaii is verified to have weighed over 1,800 pounds. It was caught on rod and reel but was not eligible for record status because more than one angler handled the tackle. Striped Marlin, the premier billfish of California, lack the great heft of Blues and Blacks but are even more acrobatic and, when matched to lighter tackle, are just as much of an angling handful. The same can be said of the Pacific Sailfish and the uncommon Spearfish. The Broadbill Swordfish stands apart from the other billfishes, both scientifically and as an angling prize. Historically a reluctant biter, the Broadbill was classed as the greatest challenge of all for many years. Now, even though a more effective fishing method has been worked out (night fishing), the challenge remains about as great, due to the depletion of Swordfish stocks by commercial longliners.

The Billfishes

Black Marlin

Blue Marlin

Sailfish

Shortbill Spearfish

Striped Marlin

Swordfish

Black Marlin

Makaira indica

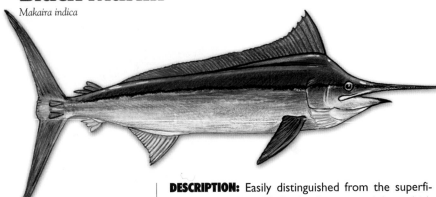

OTHER NAMES:

Aguja Negro
Marlin Negro
A'u

RANGE: *From Baja California, Mexico, to Panama; occasionally Hawaii.*

WHERE TO FISH: *Blacks roam the open sea, following currents and schools of bait, and lingering in good feeding territory such as dropoffs and sea mounts. Anglers and crews working out of popular ports have learned productive areas in their neighborhoods, but a Black might strike at any time just about anywhere in deep water.*

DESCRIPTION: Easily distinguished from the superficially similar Blue Marlin by the pectoral fins, which extend rigidly out from the body and cannot be folded. The body is very deep and head is "humped;" that is, sloping abruptly from the dorsal fin to the base of the bill. The bill itself is stout and proportionately shorter than that of the Blue Marlin. Color is generally dark blue to black above and silvery or white on the sides. Stripes are rare and faint.

SIZE: Averages 200-300 pounds. Many fish weighing between 500 and 700 pounds are caught along the Tropical American coast, especially in Panama, and a few over 1,000 pounds have been landed. The potential may be as high as a ton. World record 1,560 pounds.

FOOD VALUE: Very good but sportsmen release their catches.

GAME QUALITIES: For strength and jumping ability the Black Marlin is unsurpassed, and its rigid pectorals act somewhat like planers when it dives deep, thus creating an extra burden for the poor angler's back.

TACKLE: Only heavy gear will do. Eighty-pound-test line is standard, although 50 is adequate for the average run of fish and 130 is by no means too much for really big ones. Fighting chairs are standard on big-game boats; however, a reasonable alternative is heavy standup tackle, properly harnessed to the angler.

LURES AND BAITS: Best of all baits is a live Bonito weighing 5 pounds or more. Rigged natural baits also work well—Mackerel, Bonito, Dolphin and others. Because Blacks are usually fished in a rather defined area, such as the fabled reef off Pinas Bay, Panama, offshore trolling lures are probably less popular than natural baits, but are also effective.

Blue Marlin

Makaira nigricans

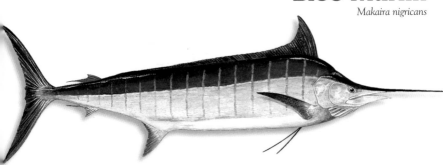

DESCRIPTION: Pectoral fins are relatively short and fold flat against the body—a sure distinguishing feature from the Black Marlin. Although the Blue's coloration can vary, the most common phase is dark blue, almost black on the dorsal surface and upper sides, shading to whitish on the lower portions of the body. Usually, several vertical stripes are noticeable, and sometimes these are quite vivid. In Black Marlin the stripes are faint, if present at all. Occasionally, in a very large Blue, the dark upper areas will look smaller and lighter. Such specimens seem to have an overall silvery appearance, and because of this they were once thought to be a separate species—the "Silver Marlin"—now known to be non-existent.

SIZE: The equal or superior of the Black Marlin in size, Blues might run anywhere from less than 200 pounds to more than 1,000, with a top potential of a ton or more. Most catches fall in the 300- to 600-pound range. World record 1,376 pounds (Pacific).

FOOD VALUE: Very good but generally released by sportsmen.

GAME QUALITIES: A supremely challenging fish for any angler and crew. Combines great strength and stamina with a flair for magnificent leaps.

TACKLE: Heavy trolling gear with lines testing 80 or 130 pounds. Experts sometimes use 50-pound lines.

LURES AND BAITS: While live and rigged natural baits work very well and were once the standards, many anglers now fast-troll large offshore lures when seeking Blue Marlin, figuring that the more territory they cover the more likely they are to encounter the prize fish.

OTHER NAMES:

Pacific Blue Marlin
Aguja Azul
Marlin Azul
A'u
Kajiki

RANGE: Mexico to Panama; Hawaii. Also rarely seen off southern California.

WHERE TO FISH: Perhaps even more than other Marlins, blues roam widely in the open sea. They are most likely to be encountered where converging currents, bottom structure, or other conditions tend to concentrate small Tuna, Dolphin (Mahi Mahi) and the other schooling fish on which they mostly feed. Again, boat captains at every marina in Marlin country choose the most likely fishing areas from experience.

Sailfish

Istiophorus platypterus

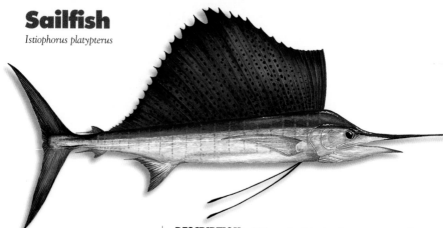

OTHER NAMES:

Pacific Sailfish
Pez Vela
A'u Lepe

RANGE: *From Baja California, Mexico, and the Gulf of California to Panama and, less commonly, southern California and Hawaii.*

WHERE TO FISH: *The deep sea, but usually in the vicinity of reef edges, islands, rips or dropoffs.*

DESCRIPTION: Although this is the same species as the Atlantic Sail, the Pacific version averages considerably larger and is slightly different in superficial appearance, being darker, more vividly striped and with a more brassy sheen. The magnificent sail-like dorsal fin sets it apart from the other billfishes. The bill is narrow and sharply pointed.

SIZE: In most parts of its range it averages 60-80 pounds. Fish over 100 pounds are not at all rare, and the potential is to more than 200. World record 221 pounds (Pacific).

FOOD VALUE: Good but sportsmen release their catches.

GAME QUALITIES: Spectacular, highly acrobatic fighter on light tackle; a great fish for the camera.

TACKLE: The standard is light ocean trolling gear with lines testing 12 to 50 pounds. Casting tackle can also be effective and a large cult of fly fishermen now chase this species with outstandingly consistent success in Central America—particularly off Guatemala, Costa Rica and Panama.

LURES AND BAITS: The Pacific Sail is such a cooperative striker on just about any rigged natural bait, or even a trolled lure, that live bait seldom is used. Fly fishermen lure the fish close by trolling a hookless decoy bait or lure called a "teaser" and then casting an oversize streamer or popper fly. The few anglers who prefer spinning or baitcasting gear for this sport get action with lures such as popping plugs, weighted streamers or molded plastic squids.

Shortbill Spearfish

Tetrapturus angustirostris

DESCRIPTION: Color is dark blue above; blue splattered with brown on the sides; silvery white below. The first dorsal fin is blue, with the other fins brown. The dorsal fin is higher and longer than that of the Striped Marlin, but not nearly so high as to be mistaken for a Sail. Per its name, the bill is very short—virtually not a bill at all.

SIZE: Most catches run 20-40 pounds; maximum is perhaps 100 pounds. World record 74 pounds, 8 ounces.

FOOD VALUE: Good.

GAME QUALITIES: A fine fighter on light line, although usually less acrobatic than Sailfish or Striped Marlin.

TACKLE: Ideal would be light trolling gear with 12- or 20-pound-test line, but most are taken with heavier tackle intended for bigger game.

LURES AND BAITS: Spearfish feed on small school fish and squid, and are susceptible to any small baits or lures used for Sailfish.

OTHER NAMES:

**Pez Aguja
Hebi**

RANGE: *Reasonably common in Hawaiian waters but an infrequent catch along the Pacific Coast from central California to Panama.*

WHERE TO FISH: *Seldom targeted but usually encountered around schools of Tuna or other small pelagic fishes.*

Striped Marlin

Tetrapturus audax

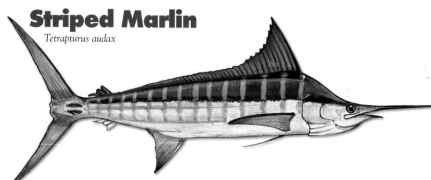

OTHER NAMES:

Nairagi
A'u

RANGE: *Southern California to Panama. Also Hawaii. This is the star attraction of the California Marlin fishery.*

WHERE TO FISH: *Apparently more migratory than other Marlins. Stripes are seasonal targets in most areas where they're fished. In California, the main season covers the summer and fall but can extend into early winter. In tropical areas where other Marlins are year-around residents, Stripers often come and go. At any rate, they follow schools of bait, such as Anchovy, Saury and Squid. Fishermen either concentrate their efforts around surfacing bait schools, or cover lots of ground by trolling.*

DESCRIPTION: Stripes are more vivid and more colorful than those of other Marlins, ranging from white to purple. The dorsal fin is high and sharply peaked and the tail is large and sickle-shaped. Overall coloration is dark blue above, fading to white on the lower sides. The bill is long and pointed, much like that of a Sailfish.

SIZE: Averages 200 pounds or so, but 300-pounders are rare prizes. Maximum potential is probably not much more than 400.

FOOD VALUE: Good but should be released.

GAME QUALITIES: Probably the wildest jumper of the Marlins, it is a light-tackle opponent of top rank.

TACKLE: Light ocean trolling gear with line of 20- to 30-pound test. Twelve-pound can be used in experienced hands, while for casual anglers 50-pound is not too heavy for great sport. Striped Marlin are rather easily hooked by fly fishermen in the manner described for Sailfish, but once hooked the comparison ends. A Striped Marlin of average size may struggle for hours against fly tackle, and so nearly all flyrod billfishermen are content to stick to their Sails.

LURES AND BAITS: Rigged natural baits, such as fish strips and squids are traditional, but high-speed lures have pretty much taken over in California and in many tropical areas where the Striped Marlin is heavily fished.

Swordfish

Xiphias gladius

DESCRIPTION: The Broadbill is a chunky and powerfully built fish with a high, crescent-shaped dorsal fin and broadly forked tail. The pectoral fins are also large and lunate. The distinguishing feature, however, is the huge bill or sword—much longer and wider than the bills of Marlins and Sailfish. The eye is also very large. Color is mostly dark brown to purple, with whitish undersides.

SIZE: Historically, from 100 to more than 1,000 pounds; however, relentless and virtually unregulated commercial longlining has lowered the average to under 50 pounds. World record 1,182 pounds.

FOOD VALUE: Among the very best, which is helping skid the species toward endangered status.

GAME QUALITIES: The Broadbill is not as wildly acrobatic as the Blue Marlin, but is an equally powerful and rugged fighter that can get off some spectacular jumps.

TACKLE: Although big fish are now quite rare, Swordfish are hooked so seldom that anyone who fishes for them is advised to use at least 50-pound line, matched to good ocean-trolling or standup tackle.

BAITS: The best Swordfish bait always has been a large, rigged natural squid, but live and rigged baitfishes also have taken lots of fish. Historically, anglers in California went after swords by searching for fish that were "finning out" on the surface, and then pulling trolled baits in front of them, in the often fruitless hope of getting a strike. This approach is still practiced to a greatly reduced extent, but drifting at night is the tactic now most likely to produce a Broadbill. The majority of strikes are delivered at 100 feet or deeper. Although night fishing has worked pretty well wherever it has been tried anywhere in the world, the scarcity of Swordfish at this writing has virtually killed off any concentrated fishing effort everywhere except southern Florida.

OTHER NAMES:

Broadbill
Pez Espada
Shutome
A'u-Ku

RANGE: *Central California to Panama. Also Hawaii.*

WHERE TO FISH: *The deep sea.*

When it comes to brutish power on a pound-for-pound basis, Jacks go to the head of the class. The Jack clan is a huge one, containing perhaps even more species of interest to anglers than the Mackerels but, as a group, they rank regrettably low in angler esteem. And yet, some species of Jacks are among the most beloved of sport fishes. Does that sound contradictory? Of course. But the reason is that the "prestigious" types all wear some name other than "Jack." To Californians, the obvious example is the Yellowtail, a most splendid fish, whether on the end of a line or on the table. But in some waters of the world, the Yellowtail and closely similar species are called "Amberjacks" and traditionally viewed as second-class citizens of the deep. Although that attitude is changing rapidly, it is still pretty common. The spectacular African Pompano is another highly prized Jack of a different label, as are, for that matter, several more Pompanos. In Hawaii, a huge and highly prized fish that goes by either the local name, Ulua, or the Australian name, Giant Trevally, is, of course, a Jack. This sort of name-prejudice has so enraged the Jack Crevalle, Black Jack, Blue Jack and other Jacks named Jack that they are always belligerent and ready to pick a rough-and-tumble fight with any fisherman. One fish in this chapter—the Roosterfish—is not a Jack by either name or classification, but is included with the group because of similar habits and characteristics. It was, in fact, once classified as a Jack before being placed in a family of its own.

Chapter 3

The Jacks

African Pompano
Almaco Jack
Bigeye Trevally
Bigeye Scad
Black Jack
Bluefin Trevally
Gaftopsail Pompano
Golden Jack
Green Jack
Jack Mackerel
Leatherjack
Mexican Scad
Pacific Crevalle Jack
Pacific Lookdown
Pacific Permit
Paloma Pompano
Pilotfish
Rainbow Runner
Roosterfish
Threadfin Jack
Ulua
Yellowtail

African Pompano

Alectis ciliaris

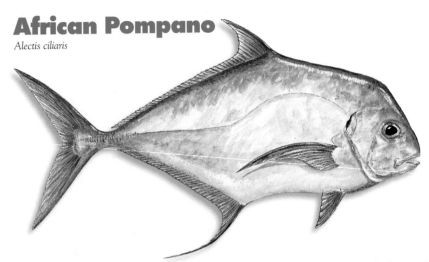

OTHER NAMES:

Threadfish
Threadfin
Ulua kīhikihi
Flechudo

RANGE: Mexico to Panama; also Hawaii.

WHERE TO FISH: The best fishing is found around deep reef and sharp offshore dropoffs, but they are also taken on shallow reefs and around inshore rocks and pinnacles. Young Threadfins sometimes are encountered drifting with weeds far offshore.

DESCRIPTION: The adult is a large, vertically flattened fish with bright pearlescent sides and a sharply sloping head. In juveniles the forward rays of the dorsal and anal fins are very long and threadlike, and these "streamers" sometimes hang on into early adulthood, although they usually are lost as the fish grows. These small "Threadfish" were once thought to be a different species.

SIZE: Adults are common at 15-30 pounds and grow to at least 50 pounds. World record 50 pounds, 8 ounces.

FOOD VALUE: Excellent.

GAME QUALITIES: The African fights much like other big Jacks, but uses its flat side to even greater advantage, and exhibits a peculiar, circling tactic that puts the angler to a rough test. All in all, it is one of the toughest light-tackle battlers.

TACKLE: Most are caught by fishing deep in the vicinity of reefs or dropoffs with stout spinning or bait-casting tackle or light ocean gear. Some are taken by trolling with the same gear. They generally hang too deep to interest fly fishermen, although a few have been caught, either by blind-fishing with fast-sinking lines over spots known to be productive, or casting to fish lured to the surface with live chum.

LURES AND BAITS: A variety of heavy leadhead jigs will work, especially if trimmed with silvery Mylar. Metallic jigs are also good. Sardines and similar small fish are the live baits of choice. Africans caught trolling most often take weighted feather-and-rigged-bait combinations, or big diving plugs.

Almaco Jack

Seriola rivoliana

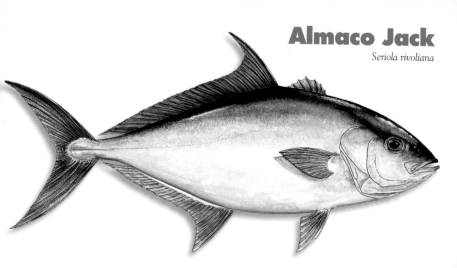

DESCRIPTION: Although rather similar to the Yellow-tail in appearance, there should be no cause for confusion. The body of the Almaco is deeper and more compressed. Also, the dorsal and anal fins are sickle-shaped and proportionately longer.

SIZE: Common from 10 to about 40 pounds; sometimes to 100 or more, but maximum appears to be less than that of the Yellowtail. World record 132 pounds.

FOOD VALUE: Excellent.

GAME QUALITIES: As tough as the Yellowtail.

TACKLE: Spinning, baitcasting and light ocean tackle with lines up to 30-pound test are ideal; however, heavier gear can also be sporting.

LURES AND BAITS: Small live fish are seldom refused. Jigs work too, when yo-yoed vertically near the bottom.

OTHER NAMES:

Pacific Amberjack
Longfin
 Amberjack
Pez Fuerte

RANGE: *Southern California to Panama.*

WHERE TO FISH: *Nearly always hooked over deep reefs or deep rocky shorelines.*

Bigeye Trevally

Caranx sexfasciatus

OTHER NAMES:

Bigeye Jack
Horse-eye Jack
Pake Ulua

RANGE: *Southern Baja California, Mexico, to Panama.*

WHERE TO FISH: *Not so widely scattered as the Crevalle, this is more of a clear-water species, found over the reefs and near the beaches; also in channels, bays and harbors where the water is not too turbid. Feeds largely at night, although many are caught by day.*

DESCRIPTION: Again, traveling anglers probably won't be able to distinguish this fish from the Horse-Eye Jack of Atlantic waters. The body color is blue to green on top and silvery or white below. The fins, including the tail, are black. Looks much like the Crevalle in silhouette but the head is not so blunt. Has hard scutes forward of tail. As the name indicates, the eyes are very large.

SIZE: Commonly up to 6 pounds and may reach nearly 20 pounds. World record 31 pounds, 8 ounces.

FOOD VALUE: Fair.

GAME QUALITIES: Great power and stubbornness, and especially strong in water deep enough so that its flat sides can be used to advantage.

TACKLE: Good target for all light tackle—spinning, baitcasting and fly.

LURES AND BAITS: Surface plugs often provide spectacular hits. Jigs and spoons produce well. Live baitfish are fine, of course, but the Bigeye will also take cutbaits.

Bigeye Scad

Selar crumenophthalmus

DESCRIPTION: The body is cylindrical and the tail forked. Hard scutes are present on the caudal peduncle. Color is steel blue above and on the sides; silvery below. The eye is very large.

SIZE: Less than 1 foot.

FOOD VALUE: Good, but usually used for bait.

GAME QUALITIES: Good fighter for its size.

TACKLE: Anglers often catch them at night, either deliberately as potential bait, or while still-fishing for other species. In either case, light spinning tackle is generally used.

LURES AND BAITS: They respond well to small jigs, often tied in tandem or series, but natural baits are always productive—tiny live or dead fish, shrimp, or little strips of squid.

OTHER NAMES:

Goggle-eye
Purse-eyed Scad
Ojoton

RANGE: Baja California, Mexico, to Panama.

WHERE TO FISH: Huge schools may be encountered from surf area to well offshore; also enters river mouths and bays but much prefers clear outside waters.

Black Jack

Caranx lugubris

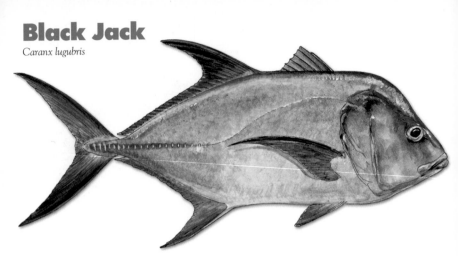

OTHER NAMES:

Jurel Negro
Brown Jack

RANGE: *Mexico to Costa Rica.*

WHERE TO FISH: *Species sticks to ocean waters and is most commonly encountered by anglers over reef dropoffs and in areas surrounding coastal islands and rocks.*

DESCRIPTION: The name says it. Body color is black or dark gray and the fins are also dark. Similar in shape to the Bigeye Trevally but somewhat deeper in the body.

SIZE: Common at 8-20 pounds; can reach perhaps 40 pounds. World record 39 pounds, 9 ounces.

FOOD VALUE: Fair.

GAME QUALITIES: Like all the Jacks, a strong but not a showy fighter.

TACKLE: Usually caught on ocean trolling gear, but is a good target for spinning and baitcasters.

LURES AND BAITS: Trolled feathers, spoons and small rigged baits take most of these fish. Surface plugs and fast-moving jigs work well for casters. Live small fish, preferably quite active, are the best natural baits.

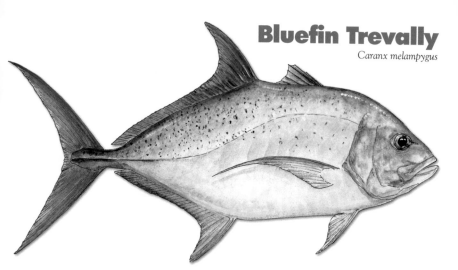

Bluefin Trevally

Caranx melampygus

DESCRIPTION: The striking color ranges from powdery blue to blue-green with a liberal sprinkling of small black dots. The fins are blue.

SIZE: Varies widely. Small ones of about 4-10 pounds are common wherever this fish occurs, but 25-pounders are common too and the potential is to 50 or more. World record 26 pounds, 7 ounces.

FOOD VALUE: Excellent.

GAME QUALITIES: Typically tough—much strength and stamina.

TACKLE: A fine foe for light spinning, baitcasting and occasionally fly gear. Larger ones will put ocean trolling tackle to a test.

LURES AND BAITS: Small spoons, jigs, topwater plugs. For fly fishing try silvery streamer flies and small popping bugs, worked as fast as possible. Small live fish. Sardines or Anchovies are almost sure bets as natural bait.

OTHER NAMES:

Blue Crevalle
Blue Jack
Bluefin Jack
Cobalt Jack
Omilu
Hoshi Ulua

RANGE: *Mexico to Panama; also Hawaii.*

WHERE TO FISH: *Clear-water coastlines around rocks, points and small islands.*

Gafftopsail Pompano

Trachinotus rhodopus

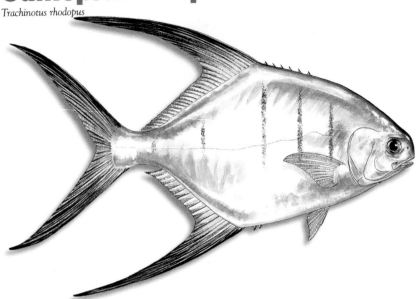

OTHER NAMES:

Paloma
Palometa
Pampanito

RANGE: *Southern California to Panama.*

WHERE TO FISH: *Gentle surf and sandy flats; also around shallow rocky reefs near shorelines.*

DESCRIPTION: Long streamers running off the dorsal and anal fins make identification easy, as do the vertical bars, which do not appear on other Pompanos. Fin color can vary from yellow to dark red.

SIZE: Most weigh a pound or less; tops is perhaps 3 or 4 pounds. World record 2 pounds, 14 ounces.

FOOD VALUE: Excellent.

GAME QUALITIES: Top-rank on appropriate light tackle. Fights as hard as a Jack of similar size but uncorks longer and zippier runs.

TACKLE: Light spinning gear is ideal; also a good target for sight-fishing with fly tackle at times.

LURES AND BAITS: By far the best natural baits are small crabs and other crustaceans, preferably live but acceptable dead. They are usually very spooky but will take jigs or sinking flies, worked slowly along soft bottom.

Golden Jack

Gnathanodon speciosus

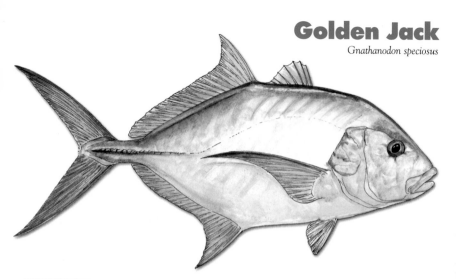

DESCRIPTION: Juveniles show several dark vertical stripes—alternately broad and narrow—on a gold background. Adults have dark backs with yellow or gold sides and are stripeless. Fins are gold on both adults and juveniles. The mouth is protractile.

SIZE: Striped specimens run to 3 or 4 pounds. Adults frequently weigh 10 or 12 pounds and can grow to 30 or more.

FOOD VALUE: Good.

GAME QUALITIES: Rugged but seems not quite as strong as the Crevalle and other Jacks.

TACKLE: Though usually caught incidentally to other fishing, Golden Jack often make fine targets of opportunity for spinning and baitcasting gear.

LURES AND BAITS: Best lures for juveniles are bucktail or plastic-tail jigs, worked slowly near bottom. Larger fish will hit a variety of cast and trolled lures, as well as natural fish and crustacean baits, live or cut.

OTHER NAMES:

**Golden Trevally
Striped Jack
Yellow Ulua**

RANGE: *Baja California, Mexico, to Panama; also Hawaii.*

WHERE TO FISH: *Bays and open shorelines, usually over shallow, soft bottom where it grubs for crustaceans. But it also feeds on small fish and is common in deeper water, often around sharks or other large marine animals.*

Green Jack

Caranx caballus

OTHER NAMES:

Green Runner
Blue Runner
Cocinero

RANGE: *Southern California to Panama.*

WHERE TO FISH: *Roams in schools, usually following small, schooling baitfishes. May show up anywhere from outside waters to bays and river mouths.*

DESCRIPTION: Trimmer body than most other Jacks. Color is blue to green on back and silvery on sides and belly. A dark spot is on the gill cover. This is another Atlantic look-alike (Blue Runner, *C. crysos*).

SIZE: Most run a pound or less, but they can reach perhaps 6 pounds. World record 6 pounds, 3 ounces.

FOOD VALUE: Good.

GAME QUALITIES: Outstanding fighter for its size; strong and dogged.

TACKLE: Light spinning and baitcasting gear.

LURES AND BAITS: Small bucktail or plastic-tail jigs are probably best. Spoons and small plugs work well. Nearly any natural bait of proper size—live or dead, fish or shellfish, is usually acceptable.

Jack Mackerel

Trachurus symmetricus

DESCRIPTION: The long, slender body is greenish on top, silvery on the sides. Scales along the lateral line are enlarged. Black spot marks the gill cover.

SIZE: Averages around 6-8 inches; grows to perhaps 18 inches.

FOOD VALUE: Good whether fresh, smoked or canned, but huge numbers are used as bait.

GAME QUALITIES: The fight isn't too great but the action often is hot.

TACKLE: Light spinning and fly tackle.

LURES AND BAITS: Live small baitfish, shrimp or small strips of fish and squid do well. For lures, multi-hooked Sabiki bait-catching rigs will take plenty. Or try small jigs, either cast or trolled.

OTHER NAMES:

**California
   Horse Mackerel
Charrito**

RANGE: *Alaska to southern Baja California, Mexico and the Gulf of California; occasionally wanders much farther south.*

WHERE TO FISH: *Just about everywhere. Thick schools of Jack Mackerel range from close inshore to hundreds of miles out. Small ones are mainstays at many piers and other onshore fishing spots. In open water, look for surface activity to give away the schools.*

Leatherjack

Oligoplites sp.

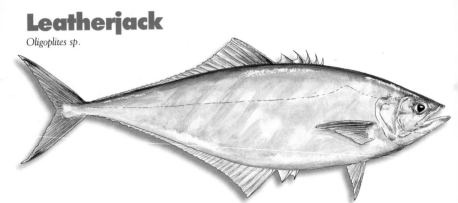

OTHER NAMES:

Leatherjacket
Zapatero

RANGE: *Baja California, Mexico, to Panama.*

WHERE TO FISH: *Not targeted by sportsmen, Leatherjacks are nevertheless caught quite often, usually when mixing with Mackerel, Jacks or other game species feeding in schools of small baitfish. So handle with care!*

DESCRIPTION: Our coverage area includes three similar species with little apparent difference to anglers—especially in regard to the sharp little spines at the front of the dorsal fin, which can deal the inattentive fisherman a burning, lingering wound. All three types are rather flat, streamlined and silvery, with forked tails.

SIZE: Large by comparison with the Atlantic type, specimens ranging from 12 inches to as much as 2 feet are common. World record 3 pounds, 8 ounces.

FOOD VALUE: Poor.

GAME QUALITIES: Not very strong, but can be acrobatic on light line.

TACKLE: Casting gear.

LURES AND BAITS: Small baitfish, jigs, spoons and small plugs are all eagerly taken.

Mexican Scad

Decapterus scombrinus

DESCRIPTION: Longer and slimmer than the Bigeye Scad, and marked by a brown or red strip down the side. Has unusual tiny finlets above and below the caudal peduncle.

SIZE: Usually 6-12 inches.

FOOD VALUE: Not bad, but usually used as bait.

GAME QUALITIES: Good strength but small size.

TACKLE: Light Spinning.

LURES AND BAITS: Tiny jigs and multi-hooked bait-catching rigs.

OTHER NAMES:

Caballa
Mexicana
Jurel Fino

RANGE: Central California to Panama.

WHERE TO FISH: Hard to pin down. Roams the open sea in large schools from close in to far offshore. Often found by activity of other fish striking the schools.

Pacific Crevalle Jack

Caranx caninus

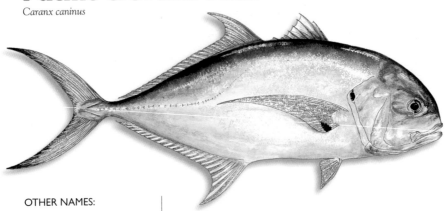

OTHER NAMES:

Jurel

RANGE: *Southern California to Panama.*

WHERE TO FISH: *Jacks are always on the move and can be encountered anywhere: the open sea; the surf and shorelines; shallow bays and estuaries; even far up coastal streams into fresh water.*

DESCRIPTION: Anglers who have fished both oceans can't tell this fellow from the Atlantic Crevalle, *C. hippos*, and some scientists can't either, believing they are one and the same. The body is deep and compressed. The head is blunt and there is a black spot on the rear edge of the gill cover. The color is dirty yellow with whitish undersides. Hard scutes present just forward of the tail.

SIZE: Common in many sizes from a couple of pounds to 20 pounds or more. Maximum potential is around 50 pounds. World record 39 pounds.

FOOD VALUE: Fair; most of the flesh is red.

GAME QUALITIES: Few fish are any tougher—or less spectacular. Long runs and powerful, circular, throbbing resistance are their trademarks.

TACKLE: Anything goes, but stout rods and fairly heavy lines can save the angler a little time that he'd rather spend chasing something more prestigious.

LURES AND BAITS: Any sort of live fish, shrimp or crab. Best artificials are noisy surface plugs and fast-whipped bucktail or baittail jigs.

Pacific Lookdown

Selene oerstedii

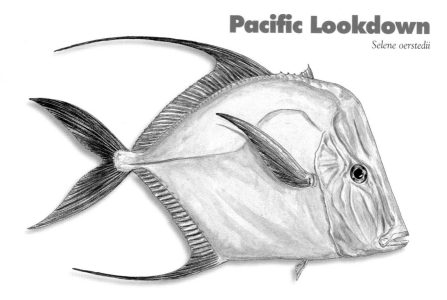

DESCRIPTION: This and a similar species—the Pacific Moonfish (*S. peruviana*)—are flat, blunt-headed, silvery fish of similar size, appearance and habits. They are often found in company with each other, especially at night around lights. The Lookdown has a sloping, concave head and long streamers running off the dorsal and anal fins. The head of the Moonfish is less blunted than that of the Lookdown, and all its fins are short.

SIZE: Usually less than a pound, but both types often reach 2 pounds and can run to 3 or 4 on rare occasion.

FOOD VALUE: Both species are tasty panfish.

GAME QUALITIES: Aggressive strikers and good fighters for their size, they are prone to running in circles and resisting with their broad sides. Small Lookdown and Moonfish make good night-fishing baits for Corvina, Snook and Snapper.

TACKLE: Ultralight or very light spinning and fly tackle.

LURES AND BAITS: Tiny live baitfish or live shrimp are seldom refused, but tiny jigs, spoons and flies are also very productive around lights at night. Daytime catches are largely incidental to other endeavors.

OTHER NAMES:

Horse-head
Jorobado

RANGE: Southern California to Panama; common from southern Baja California southward.

WHERE TO FISH: Nearly anywhere in shallow coastal waters, but most common around bridge and dock pilings, navigation markers, and in channels and canals, where they frequently gather under shoreside lights at night.

Pacific Permit

Trachinotus kennedyi

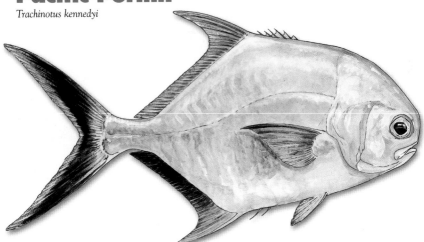

OTHER NAMES:

**Pacific Pompano
Longfin Pompano
Blackblotch Permit**

RANGE: *Southern Baja California, Mexico, to Panama.*

WHERE TO FISH: *Adults and juveniles feed in the surf and shallow water of bays, mostly on shellfish.*

DESCRIPTION: Similar in appearance to the Atlantic Permit, although does not grow nearly so large. Overall color is metallic, usually silver but often goldish. There is a black blotch on the inner side of the pectoral fin. The head is blunter than that of the Pacific Pompano.

SIZE: Averages 3-4 pounds; sometimes reaches 10 pounds or more.

FOOD VALUE: Excellent.

GAME QUALITIES: Outstanding. Battle features long runs in shallow water and Jack-like throbbing if deep water is reached.

TACKLE: Spinning and baitcasting.

LURES AND BAITS: Good natural baits include small crabs or pieces of cut crab and clam. Small jigs, hopped slowly on bottom are the best artificial lures.

Paloma Pompano

Trachinotus paitensis

DESCRIPTION: The overall coloration is greenish or bluish above and silver on the sides. The dorsal and caudal fins are dark; the anal fin yellow. No hard scutes.

SIZE: Averages a pound or 2; might reach 5 or 6 pounds.

FOOD VALUE: Ranks among the best.

GAME QUALITIES: Also top-rank. Fights as hard as a Jack of similar size but gets off longer and zippier runs.

TACKLE: Light spinning gear is ideal. Not easily targetable by fly fishermen but sometimes provide good shots for anglers walking a beach or wading.

LURES AND BAITS: By far the best natural baits are small crabs and other crustaceans, preferably live but acceptable dead. They are ready strikers of small artificial jigs, the favorite being quarter-ounce or half-ounce models with short nylon skirts. Fly fishermen can catch Pompano with flies, tied with epoxy heads or lead eyes for fast-sinking.

OTHER NAMES:

Pacific Pompano

RANGE: *Baja California, Mexico, to Panama; straggles to California.*

WHERE TO FISH: *Most are caught from the surf or from shallow flats in bays and around outlets, but they also run the edges of channels, especially channels through grass flats.*

Pilotfish

Naucrates ductor

OTHER NAMES:

**Pez Piloto
Romero**

RANGE: *British Columbia to Panama.*

WHERE TO FISH: *Offshore waters, often accompanying sharks and other large animals, seemingly as pilots, hence the name.*

DESCRIPTION: The shape is slender with tapering head. The body is marked by wide, dark bands and the fins are also banded. Note that there is no diagonal line through the eye, which means that fish is not a member of the Amberjack group, as some anglers believe. The superficially similar Banded Rudderfish, *Seriola zonata*, is a small Amberjack that is confined to the Atlantic.

SIZE: Usually a foot or so; grows to 2 feet.

FOOD VALUE: Good, if fish is large enough.

GAME QUALITIES: Good on light tackle; gives the fight of a typical small Jack.

TACKLE: Only very light outfits can provide much sport.

LURES AND BAITS: Readily takes small jigs and streamer flies.

Rainbow Runner

Elegatis bipinnulata

DESCRIPTION: Blue and yellow full-length stripes against a blue background make this the most colorful of all jacks. The underparts are white. The head is pointed and the tail slender. There are no hard scutes on the caudal peduncle.

SIZE: Varies from a couple of pounds to 15 or 20 pounds, with individuals of roughly the same size forming large schools. World record 37 pounds, 9 ounces.

FOOD VALUE: Excellent.

GAME QUALITIES: Despite difference in shape, the Rainbow Runner is as tough for its size as any Jack, besides which, it makes faster runs and may even jump.

TACKLE AND BAITS: Most of the rare catches are made by blind trolling with heavy tackle, but if you ever get the chance to fish selectively for Rainbow Runners, you can use spinning, baitcasting and light ocean rigs. Small live fish and small rigged baits are the best bets. They can be coaxed to a jig, spoon or small swimming plug.

OTHER NAMES:

Rainbow Jack
Spanish Jack
Kamanu

RANGE: *Baja California, Mexico to Panama; also Hawaii.*

HABITAT: *The deep ocean.*

Roosterfish

Nematistius pectoralis

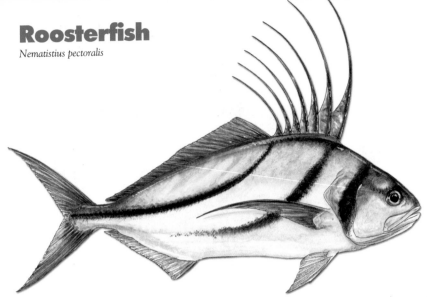

OTHER NAMES:

Gallo
Papagallo
Pez Gallo

RANGE: *Baja California, Mexico, to Panama; occasionally southern California.*

WHERE TO FISH: *Close to shore along beaches and rocky shorelines, and around the rock islands that are common over much of their range.*

DESCRIPTION: Look no further than the "rooster's comb" of elongated dorsal spines to identify this famous game species. The long spines are yellow with black tips. The back is gray or charcoal in color and the sides are silvery. Two dark stripes sweep downward and backward from the dorsal fin on each side.

SIZE: Most Roosters run from about 10 pounds to 40 or 50 pounds, but often grow much larger. World record 114 pounds.

FOOD VALUE: Good but seldom killed by sportsmen.

GAME QUALITIES: One of the premier light-tackle species of the tropics. Long, fast runners.

TACKLE: Heavy baitcasting or spinning tackle, or light ocean outfits, spooled with lines of 12- to 30-pound test are ideal in most instances, but fish ranging upwards of 60 pounds will put heavier trolling outfits to a good test. Occasionally the opportunity arises to fly-fish for Roosters, but this is a tough challenge that works best when the fish are rather small and in competitive schools.

LURES AND BAITS: Live baits top the list—either schooling baitfishes, such as Sardines and Herrings, or else small Jacks or Scads. Trolled rigged baits, along with trolled spoons, feathers and vibrating plugs are productive. Casters do best with noisy topwater plugs, worked fast and with a maximum amount of surface commotion.

Threadfin Jack

Carangoides otrynter

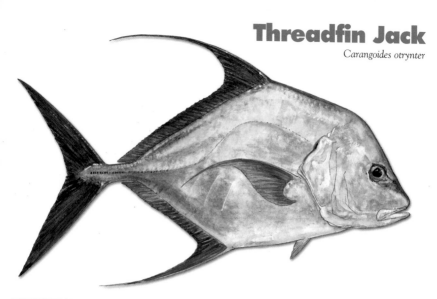

DESCRIPTION: Silvery or silvery gray overall. Forehead is sloped. First dorsal and anal spines are long and threadlike.

SIZE: From 2 to 6 pounds.

FOOD VALUE: Very good.

GAME QUALITIES: Tough fighter on light gear.

TACKLE: Spinning and baitcasting.

LURES AND BAITS: Jigs, spoons, small trolling feathers.

OTHER NAMES:

Threadfish

RANGE: Baja California, Mexico, to Panama.

WHERE TO FISH: Open water, often well offshore.

Ulua

Caranx ignobilis

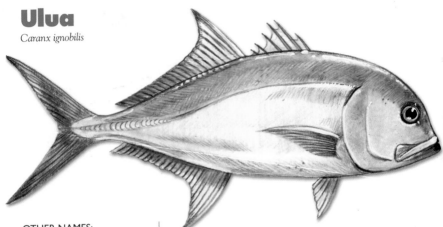

OTHER NAMES:

Giant Trevally
Pa'u'u
Turrum

RANGE: *Hawaii.*

WHERE TO FISH: *Adults roam all around the shorelines of the Hawaiian Islands, and also over reefs.*

DESCRIPTION: Head and body are dusky yellow above, gray or silvery below. The fins are dark. Head is very blunt.

SIZE: Juveniles (called Papio) range from a few inches to a few pounds, but the heaviest sportfishing interest is centered on the big boys, which frequently push 100 pounds in weight and occasionally exceed that figure by a goodly margin. The potential is to more than 150 pounds. World record 145 pounds, 8 ounces.

FOOD VALUE: Good.

GAME QUALITIES: It would be hard to imagine a tougher opponent. It has typical Jack strength and stamina, backed by enormous size.

TACKLE: Heavy surf tackle for fishing from shore; medium ocean tackle for trolling. Juveniles are caught in harbors and quiet coves on poles and light spinning gear.

LURES AND BAITS: Shore fishermen use many different baits. Octopus is very popular as are crabs and other shellfish, plus cut fish. Best fishing is at night. Diving plugs are good choices for trolling.

Yellowtail

Seriola lalandi

DESCRIPTION: The back and upper sides are dark blue or gray. The lower sides are white, and there is a yellow line at about the dividing point of dark and light. The fins are yellow.

SIZE: Averages probably 15-30 pounds, but often grows to well over 100 pounds. Maximum potential is to nearly 200 pounds. World record 114 pounds, 10 ounces.

FOOD VALUE: Excellent.

GAME QUALITIES: Among the best for long, strong resistance.

TACKLE: In California, long livebait rods with either heavy spinning or oversize casting reels get the nod from most private boat and party boat anglers. These fish are tough, however, and provide sport and challenge even with heavier standup and trolling gear, especially when fished deep in Latin American waters.

LURES AND BAITS: Live bait, either fish or squid according to place and season, is the mainstay of California party boat anglers, but many kinds of artificial lures are also used with good effect. Best probably are metallic jigs; with leadhead jigs a close second. Both draw strikes when fished deep and vertically, and the metallics are also deadly when cast at fish feeding at or near the surface and retrieved rapidly. Any sort of live fish (small Jacks and Scads are especially good) can be dropped to deep structure in other areas for an almost certain hit if Yellowtail are present.

OTHER NAMES:

Pacific Yellowtail
Pacific Amberjack
Kahala

RANGE: *British Columbia to Panama, but common only from southern California southward. They are also found in the Hawaiian Islands, although those fish may be the very similar (some scientists say identical) Greater Amberjack, S. dumerili.*

WHERE TO FISH: *Southern California and Baja stocks often school heavily in many types of surroundings, including kelp beds, near rocky reefs and deep island shorelines, and even in open water, where they gang up to feed on schools of baitfish or squid, all of which makes them a great favorite of partyboat anglers. Farther south, they most often are found hanging around deep reefs.*

The fish in this chapter have little in common except that they are all fine sport fish. Most are either the only member of their family, or else the only member of interest to Pacific anglers. A couple of exceptions are the Ladyfish and Tarpon, which are related, and the Barracudas, which are even more closely related but do not overlap in range. The Great Barracuda is not found along the mainland shores of Pacific America but only around Hawaii. Science recognizes several species of Bonefish in tropical waters of the world but they all look—and act—alike to traveling anglers who encounter them in different oceans, as well as to the International Game Fish Association, which lumps all of them together for record-keeping purposes. The Tarpon is still an oddity in the Pacific but its number and range seem to be expanding steadily. Beautiful and sporty Dolphin are pets of anglers in tropical offshore waters (except when they are stealing billfish baits). Tripletail are far less common but might be encountered, along with a school of Dolphin, around floating weeds or debris offshore. Strikingly colored, the adult California Sheepshead is among the most spectacular of bottom feeders but, unfortunately, the really big fellows are in sad decline because they need many years to grow. Finally, Sturgeon—mainly the White Sturgeon—might be considered more of a freshwater species, but is a regular target of sportsmen in bays and estuaries of the West Coast, particularly in San Francisco Bay.

Rugged Individuals

California Sheepshead

Dolphin

Great Barracuda

Green Sturgeon

Pacific Barracuda

Pacific Bonefish

Pacific Ladyfish

Tarpon

Tripletail

White Sturgeon

California Sheepshead

Semicossyphus pulcher

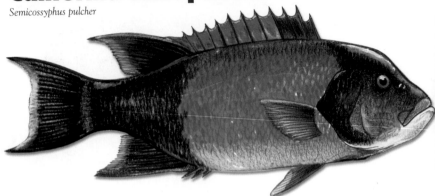

OTHER NAMES:

Vieja

RANGE: *Central California to Baja California and the Gulf of California, Mexico.*

WHERE TO FISH: *Rocky bottom, especially around kelp beds. Usually found in around 50-80 feet of water, but they are also taken near jetties as well as farther offshore by anglers after Rockfish.*

DESCRIPTION: Adult males are spectacular, with a wide pinkish or rosy band amidships, flanked by a black head and black rear section. The chin is white. The large canine teeth are also spectacular. Adult females are much smaller and of a more uniform reddish-orange color. At about a foot long, all females change to males.

SIZE: Although they can reach or exceed 30 pounds, it takes many years to reach anywhere close to that size and so really big males are now scarce. A 10- or 12-pounder now gives cause for boasting.

FOOD VALUE: Very good.

GAME QUALITIES: Depends mainly on size. Big ones are rugged foes.

TACKLE: Light bottom-fishing gear is best, but heavier tackle will be needed for deep fishing at 150 feet or more.

LURES AND BAITS: Shellfish baits are essential—crab, shrimp or trimmings from lobster and abalone.

Dolphin
Coryphaena hippurus

DESCRIPTION: The brilliantly colored Dolphin is a blaze of blue and yellow or deep green and yellow when in the water, and sometimes shows dark vertical stripes as well when excited. Small dark spots sprinkle the sides. The dorsal fin extends nearly from head to tail. The head is very blunt in males (bulls); rounded in females (cows).

SIZE: Dolphin in schools run to roughly similar size, from a couple of pounds to nearly 20 pounds at times; larger fish are loners, or else are paired—bull and cow. Big bulls often reach 50 pounds in weight and can exceed 80 pounds on rare occasion. Large cows generally top out at 40 pounds or so. World record 88 pounds.

FOOD VALUE: None better.

GAME QUALITIES: Top of the heap in any weight class—speedy, strong and acrobatic.

TACKLE: With the democratic Dolphin, anything goes, even spinning, baitcasting or fly tackle. Once a school of fish is located, casting targets can usually be kept around the boat by restrained chumming with cutbait and/or by keeping at least one hooked fish in the water at all times. Most Dolphin, though, are taken with ocean trolling tackle—light-line classes if Dolphin are the main goal; heavier classes when they fall incidentally to billfish or tuna anglers.

LURES AND BAITS: A hot school will eagerly accept jigs or, for that matter, all sorts of casting baits, including flies and popping bugs. If strikes slow down, cutbait often does the trick. Big or wise fish may insist on live baits.

OTHER NAMES:

**Dolphinfish
Dorado
Mahi Mahi**

RANGE: *Open waters from Baja California, Mexico, to Panama; also Hawaii. Sometimes taken off southern California and, very rarely, farther north.*

WHERE TO FISH: *Dolphin roam the open sea in a continuous hunt for food. Anglers seek them along rafted weedlines and around flotsam. The location of schools may also be given away by feeding birds, particularly frigate birds.*

Great Barracuda

Sphyraena barracuda

OTHER NAMES:

Kaku
Picuda

RANGE: *Hawaii is about as far east as the species is found in Pacific waters.*

WHERE TO FISH: *Juveniles frequent shallow shoreline areas. Although the big fellows prefer to lurk around reefs and dropoffs, they also venture into harbors.*

DESCRIPTION: Color is greenish or gray above, with silvery sides marked by black blotches. The body is elongated and the tail sharply forked. But the best identifier of the Great Barracuda is its pointed head and wicked-looking fangs.

SIZE: Most run from 10 to 20 pounds. Individuals up to 40 pounds are not unusual, and the potential is to 80 pounds or more. World record 84 pounds, 14 ounces.

FOOD VALUE: Excellent, but large specimens have been known to carry ciguatera poison.

GAME QUALITIES: Ranks among the most spectacular of light-tackle fighters, frequently mixing fast and fairly long runs with greyhounding jumps. It can also fight deep with good strength and stamina.

TACKLE: Its reputation has been dampened by the fact that it is often caught on tackle more suitable for large Tuna or Billfish, but if choosing Barracuda gear, one should pick rather stout spinning or baitcasting tackle or, for trolling, light classes of ocean gear.

LURES AND BAITS: Nothing beats a live fish, but many trolling and casting lures, particularly if they are shiny and fast-moving, will attract strikes from Barracuda.

Green Sturgeon

Acipenser medirostris

DESCRIPTION: Similar to the White Sturgeon but the barbels are usually closer to the mouth than to the snout. Color is dark green or olive green above, lighter green below. The snout is rather blunt and shovel-shaped.

SIZE: Can reach 7 feet and more than 300 pounds, although most catches run under 50 pounds.

FOOD VALUE: Ranks well below the White Sturgeon but is not bad smoked.

GAME QUALITIES: Size alone makes it a challenge.

TACKLE: Heavy baitcasting, light saltwater or salmon mooching outfits.

LURES AND BAITS: Shrimp, marine worms, cut fish, clams.

RANGE: *About the same as the White Sturgeons, but Greens are less plentiful.*

WHERE TO FISH: *In estuaries, bays and lower reaches of rivers. The Green Sturgeon does not roam nearly as far inland as the White Sturgeon.*

Pacific Barracuda

Syphyraena argentea

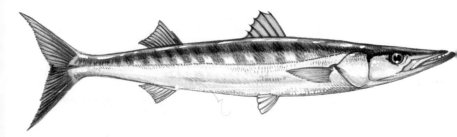

OTHER NAMES:

California Barracuda
Picuda
Agujon

RANGE: *Alaska to southern Baja California, Mexico, but fished most heavily off southern California. Two very similar species occur in Latin America—the Lucas or Gulf Barracuda (S. lucasana) in Baja California, Mexico, and the Mexican Barracuda (S. ensis) from Baja to Panama.*

WHERE TO FISH: *From shore to moderate distances offshore, usually near the surface and often around kelp beds.*

DESCRIPTION: Shape is thin and pike-like. Color is bluish or brownish on top and silvery on the sides.

SIZE: Averages 3-6 pounds; sometimes exceeds 10 pounds. Potential is to more than 20 pounds. World record 26 pounds, 8 ounces.

FOOD VALUE: Very good.

GAME QUALITIES: Hard striker and swift runner.

TACKLE: Light gear is best—spinning, baitcasting and even fly tackle at times. Heavier spinning and light ocean tackle is also sporting and a good choice for party boat or pier fishing.

LURES AND BAITS: Barracuda love Anchovies and other live small fish. They also are good strikers on metallic jigs, feather or plastic-tail jigs, spoons, swimming plugs and long streamer flies.

Pacific Bonefish

Albula neoguinaica

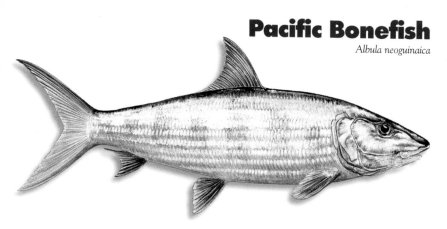

DESCRIPTION: To most anglers, a Bonefish is a Bonefish, and so any Pacific specimen, wherever taken, is often considered to be the famous Atlantic Bonefish, *Albula vulpes*. They all do look much alike but, in actuality, two different species make up the major portion of the Pacific fishery—the Sharpjaw Bonefish (*A. neoguinaica*) and the Roundjaw (*A. glossodonta*). The latter has an angled or rounded lower jaw. The lower jaw of the former is pointed.

SIZE: All three major species named above may sometimes exceed 10 pounds and possibly grow to around 20 pounds; however, the Sharpjaw averages considerably smaller than the other two.

FOOD VALUE: Bonefish are seldom kept by sportsmen. They are indeed very bony.

GAME QUALITIES: The long-distance running capability of a Bonefish in a foot or so of water is legendary. In deep water, the battle is rough and bullish.

TACKLE: Classic sight fishing for Bonefish makes use of spinning outfits with lines up to 10-pound test. Light baitcasting outfits can also be effective in practiced hands. Bonefish rank among the top favorites of fly fishermen, whose standard gear is an 8-weight outfit.

LURES AND BAITS: Live shrimp, small crabs, and cut pieces of shrimp, crab or other shellfish make the best natural baits. Most productive spinning lures are horizontally flattened jigs, often called skimmers, weighing up to ¼ ounce. These plane upward on the retrieve and keep the hook upright. Most flyrodders prefer very small flies.

OTHER NAMES:

Macabi
O'io

RANGE: *Hawaii and the west coast of the Americas from northern California to Panama. Bonefish are rarities north of Baja California, Mexico.*

WHERE TO FISH: *Although they stick to deep water most of the time and can be taken only by still-fishing or random casting, Bonefish regularly explore the shallows for food—and that is where most fishing for them takes place. Over mud, sand or grass flats, or near calm beaches, feeding Bonefish can be sighted and cast to. They may also gather in large schools over fairly deep, soft bottom, where their feeding stirs up patches of silt or "mud."*

Pacific Ladyfish

Elops affinis

OTHER NAMES:

Machete

RANGE: *Southern California to Panama. A very similar species, E. hawaiiensis, is found in Hawaii.*

WHERE TO FISH: *Ranges from calm outside beaches and shorelines to inlets and bays, and far up coastal streams. They seem to have no preferred surroundings, but follow wherever good feeding conditions take them—whether over shallow flats or in deep holes and channels. They love to feed at night and are common around lighted areas of piers and docks. They often gather in large schools.*

DESCRIPTION: A slender, silvery fish with deeply forked tail and large, scoop-shaped lower jaw.

SIZE: Usually 1-2 pounds, but fish weighing 3 or 4 pounds are common at times. Rarely reaches 8 pounds.

FOOD VALUE: Edible but not very appetizing. The meat is soft and also very bony.

GAME QUALITIES: One of the wildest acrobats, always getting off spectacular and frequent jumps. Larger Ladyfish are strong pullers and can uncork some surprisingly long runs.

TACKLE: Any sort of light or ultralight casting tackle, including fly, will provide great sport.

LURES AND BAITS: Most are caught on cut strips, small live fish or live shrimp by anglers fishing for something else, often Mackerel, but Ladyfish are ready strikers on most artificial lures of appropriate size. Jigs and small topwater plugs rate high, as do popping bugs and small white streamer flies.

Tarpon
Megalops atlanticus

DESCRIPTION: The back is dark green or gray, while the rest of the fish seems to be fashioned from silver. The scales are huge, the body of adult fish deep and thick, with a forked tail. Mouth is large and scoop-shaped. There is a long streamer at the rear of the dorsal fin.

SIZE: Averages 50-75 pounds but is common at 100 pounds and, in the Atlantic, sometimes exceeds 200 pounds. World record 283 pounds, 4 ounces.

FOOD VALUE: For the sportsman, none.

GAME QUALITIES: Tarpon are justly famous for the spectacle and frequency of their jumps but they also fight with strength, especially in deeper water.

TACKLE: For trolling or still-fishing, stout boat tackle with saltwater reels and lines testing at least 30 pounds draw heavy duty. But Tarpon are at their best as casting targets and all sizes of spinning, baitcasting and fly tackle get lots of play for small and medium fish. It is advisable to use at least 15-pound line on spinning and casting gear, and at least a 10-weight fly outfit with minimum 16-pound tippet. Heavy monofilament leaders (and heavy tippets for fly fishing) are required because of the Tarpon's very rough mouth—perhaps 50- or 60-pound mono for medium-size fish and 100- or 120-pound material for bigger ones.

LURES AND BAITS: Best live baits are small fish and small crabs. All Tarpon, including big ones, will take dead baits, such as a fish head or chunk of fish dunked patiently on bottom. For trolling, large jigs, spoons and swimming plugs form the usual arsenal. Casters use jigs, surface plugs, swimming plugs and plastic baits, but must remember that no fish is more moody about striking. Fly fishermen rely heavily on scissor-action feather streamers and bulky bucktail streamers.

OTHER NAMES:

Sabalo
Silver King

RANGE: *The Tarpon is an Atlantic species. Those in the Pacific—and there are surprising numbers of them by now—have migrated via the Panama Canal, spreading gradually northward over the years to estuarine areas of Panama's Pacific side. They have even been spotted in southern Costa Rica.*

WHERE TO FISH: *No Pacific fishery has yet been established, so Tarpon are largely targets of opportunity, most likely to be encountered by anglers seeking Corvina or Snook along beaches or in the mouths and lower reaches of rivers. They usually give away their presence by rolling at the surface.*

Tripletail
Lobotes surinamensis

OTHER NAMES:

Drift Fish
Leaf Fish

RANGE: *Nicaragua to Panama; occasionally encountered offshore as far north as California.*

WHERE TO FISH: *The Tripletail is a true world traveler, drifting with ocean currents in tropical and subtropical seas and occasionally spotted by offshore trollers in weedlines or alongside floating debris. In Costa Rica and Panama they are sometimes found close to shore, or in bays and ship channels, hanging close to navigation aids.*

DESCRIPTION: The shape is deep and rounded. Color varies but is usually brownish and mottled. Head is concave above the mouth. The name derives from the similarity and near juxtaposition of the dorsal, caudal and anal fins, resembling three tails.

SIZE: Usually 2-12 pounds, but it may exceed 30 pounds. World record 42 pounds, 5 ounces.

FOOD VALUE: One of the best.

GAME QUALITIES: Despite its clumsy looks, the Tripletail is a good gamefish in all respects. It willingly strikes artificial lures and its fight is characterized by frantic runs and startling jumps. Big ones in deep water are also good at bulldogging.

TACKLE: Casting tackle—fly, plug or spinning—provides the best and most spectacular sport with Tripletail, but saltwater outfits with lines up to 30-pound test are not out of place for big fish in tight places.

LURES AND BAITS: Streamer flies, plastic and bucktail jigs and mirror plugs are among the pet lures. Best natural baits are live shrimp and small live fish. Strip baits and dead shrimp are also accepted.

White Sturgeon

Acipenser transmontanus

DESCRIPTION: With their pointed snouts, underslung mouths and armor-like plate, Sturgeons are not apt to be misidentified. The White Sturgeon is brown or pale green above, dingy white below, and the fins are gray. The barbels are closer to the mouth than to the snout. No scutes are present behind the dorsal and anal fins.

SIZE: White Sturgeon in the history books have run as high as 1,800 pounds but any fish over 100 pounds is now a prize. Still, it remains possible to tangle with a 200- or 300-pounder. World record 468 pounds.

FOOD VALUE: Large fish are usually released. Sturgeon of small (but legal) size are excellent, either fresh or smoked.

GAME QUALITIES: A rugged fighter that uses strength, stamina and dirty tricks, such as rolling in the line and leader.

TACKLE: Very heavy baitcasting gear, salmon mooching tackle or light saltwater outfits. Ocean tackle is best when fishing very deep or in strong currents.

LURES AND BAITS: Only natural baits are used and there are many, so local advice is often a must. Leading the list are shrimp, small fish such as smelt and herring, marine worms, and clams.

RANGE: *Pacific Coast watersheds from southern Alaska to central California. Best and best-known fishery is in the Columbia River. Much of this fishery is confined to landlocked areas between dams, but the anadromous population below Bonneville Dam seems to be at least slightly on the upswing in the estuaries and bays of Oregon and Washington. Good fishing also is to be found in San Francisco Bay.*

WHERE TO FISH: *On bottom and very patiently. Fishing spots are largely found through local advice or by trial and error, but fish might be hooked anywhere from the shorelines and bays to the tailwaters of dams.*

Yes, all of these fish are capable of croaking and many of them do. But don't hold that against them. Consider, instead, that the family encompasses a raft of species that are not only big and beautiful but are also sport fish that hold vast appeal for anglers in virtually all coastal waters from California to South America. A blanket name for many in the family is "Corvina," and it is a name as well known to restaurant patrons as to fishermen. Note that in Spanish, the letters "v" and "b" are identical in sound, so you will often see "Corvina" and "Corbina" used interchangeably. In the angling vernacular, however, "Corbina" is generally reserved for the California Corbina, which is closely related to the Atlantic Whitings, while "Corvina" usually refers to those Pacific fishes that are in the same genus as the Atlantic Weakfish and Seatrout. Some of the Corvinas, though, grow far larger than any Atlantic Seatrout, and a couple of other Pacific Croakers—the White Sea Bass and Totuava—can grown far larger yet, potentially to upwards of 100 pounds. The California Corbina is a fixture of California surf fishing but the only Corvina that's prominent in the state is the Yellowmouth, which has successfully been introduced to the inland Salton Sea. Yes, Croakers inhabit Pacific waters in great profusion, and sometimes great confusion. However, by studying the entries in this chapter you should soon be able to distinguish among them.

The Croakers

5

Bairdiella

Black Croaker

California Corbina

Gulf Corvina

Highfin Kingcroaker

Orangemouth Corvina

Pacific Drum

Pacific Kingcroaker

Queenfish

Shortfin Corvina

Spotfin Croaker

Stolzmann's Corvina

Striped Corvina

Totuava

White Corvina

White Croaker

White Seabass

Yellowfin Croaker

Bairdiella

Bairdiella icistia

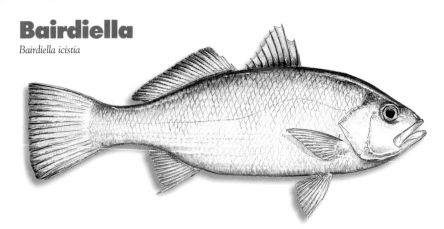

OTHER NAMES:

Romeo Croaker
Covineta

RANGE: *Gulf of California, Mexico, to Nicaragua. Strays to southern California, and has been introduced into California's Salton Sea, where it is a staple catch of sports anglers.*

WHERE TO FISH: *Close to shore around structure, in channels and in the surf. In the Salton Sea it seeks deeper water during cold weather.*

DESCRIPTION: Overall color is silvery and the mouth is small. Absence of teeth and the large spine on anal fin distinguish it from juvenile Corvinas.

SIZE: Averages around 8 inches; occasionally reaches twice that length.

FOOD VALUE: An excellent panfish.

GAME QUALITIES: Spunky but light.

TACKLE: Many are caught on poles and handlines. Ultralight spinning is ideal.

BAITS AND LURES: Not picky. Loves shrimp, marine worms, cut squid, and cut baitfish, among many others.

Black Croaker

Cheilotrema saturnum

DESCRIPTION: Deep-bodied shape is similar to that of the Atlantic Black Drum, but this fish is much smaller and has no barbels.

SIZE: Usually 12-16 inches. World record 4 pounds, 8 ounces.

FOOD VALUE: Good.

GAME QUALITIES: Good fighter but a lightweight.

TACKLE: Spinning and baitcasting gear.

BAITS AND LURES: Crabs or pieces of crab, shrimp, squid. Seldom caught on a lure.

OTHER NAMES:

**Blackspot Croaker
China Croaker
Roncacho**

RANGE: *California to northern Gulf of California, Mexico.*

WHERE TO FISH: *Rocky shoreline areas and reefs to about 100 feet.*

California Corbina

Menticirrhus undulatus

OTHER NAMES:

California Kingcroaker
California Whiting
Surffish

RANGE: *California to Panama.*

WHERE TO FISH: *Prefers sandy surf, but also found along margins of bays. Good pier fish.*

DESCRIPTION: Silvery sides with dark fins. Blunt nose with single barbel under chin. Upper lobe of tail fin is slightly elongated.

SIZE: Most run 2-4 pounds but can top 6 pounds. World record 6 pounds, 8 ounces.

FOOD VALUE: Very good.

GAME QUALITIES: Strong fighter and fairly long runner on light line.

TACKLE: Normal spinning or baitcasting gear, even fly gear, can be used in most cases, since Corvina are usually within easy casting distance of beach or shore. Surf gear may be needed where wave action is heavy.

BAITS AND LURES: Small crustaceans and marine worms work best. Small jigs bounced slowly on bottom also produce well. Flyrodders should try epoxy shrimp or other weighted flies.

Gulf Corvina

Cynoscion orthonopterus

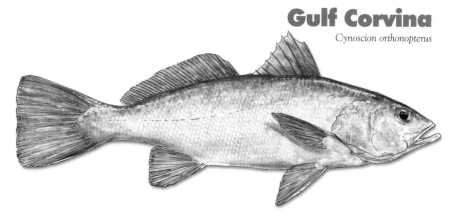

DESCRIPTION: Similar in color to the Orangemouth Corvina but the fins are yellow and the tail is square.

SIZE: Commonly caught at any weight from 5 to 20 pounds. Potential is to at least 40 pounds.

FOOD VALUE: Very good.

GAME QUALITIES: Showy and a fairly strong battler on light tackle.

TACKLE: Spinning, baitcasting or light ocean gear.

BAITS AND LURES: Live baitfish or squid. Will also hit dead baits. Many are caught trolling, and also casting with jigs, spoons and swimming plugs. Lures generally work best when fished slowly near bottom.

OTHER NAMES:

Gulf Weakfish

RANGE: *Mexico to Ecuador.*

WHERE TO FISH: *Coastal areas, bays and estuaries, and well into brackish waters of rivers.*

Highfin Kingcroaker

Menticirrhus nasus

OTHER NAMES:

Highfin Corbina

RANGE: *Southern California and Gulf of California to Panama.*

WHERE TO FISH: *Sandy surf is best, although many are caught in bays and from piers and docks.*

DESCRIPTION: The high dorsal fin is a giveaway. Color is dusky gray overall with lighter underparts. Single barbel under chin. Lower lobe of caudal fin is round.

SIZE: Can reach or exceed 2 feet, but most run 12-18 inches and weigh 1 or 2 pounds.

FOOD VALUE: Good.

GAME QUALITIES: Tough battler on light line.

TACKLE: Like the California Corbina, this fish often forages just off the beach and is easily reachable with light spinning and baitcasting gear or fly rod.

BAITS AND LURES: Any sort of crustacean, live or dead. Sight fishing is often possible and the Highfin can be coaxed into taking small jigs or epoxy flies.

Orangemouth Corvina

Cynoscion xanthulus

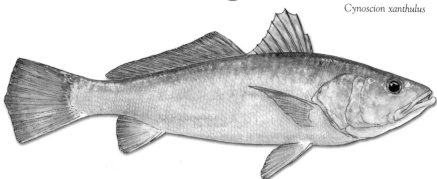

DESCRIPTION: Silvery with bluish back. Fins are yellow and the tail is convex. Prominent canine teeth. No barbels. Inside of mouth is deep yellow to orange.

SIZE: Averages 2-6 pounds or so, but 10-pounders are common and much bigger ones are not rare. Potential is to more than 50 pounds. World record 54 pounds, 3 ounces.

FOOD VALUE: Excellent.

GAME QUALITIES: A strong and showy fighter.

TACKLE: Spinning and baitcasting gear, plus light ocean tackle for trolling or live-baiting.

BAITS AND LURES: Live fish produce best, with Tilapia the top choice in the Salton Sea. Trolling with stout crankbaits is a good tactic. Casting lures include spoons and swimming plugs, but the best may be a plastic-tail leadhead jig, worked slowly over the bottom.

OTHER NAMES:

Yellowmouth Corvina

RANGE: Native to Baja California and the Gulf of California, Mexico, and south to Panama. Introduced to the Salton Sea, California, where it is now a popular target.

WHERE TO FISH: Many inshore areas, but particularly sandy areas close to points, rocks and pilings.

Pacific Drum

Larimus pacificus

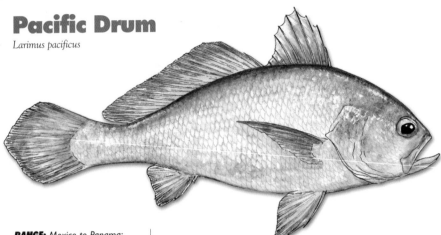

RANGE: *Mexico to Panama; rarely straggles to southern California.*

WHERE TO FISH: *Many nearshore areas and out to about 50 feet.*

DESCRIPTION: Larger eye and mouth than similar croakers. Color is silvery, sometimes with golden shading, and longitudinal stripes following scale rows on lower sides.

SIZE: Tops is about 10 inches. Most run 4 or 5 inches.

FOOD VALUE: Good but very small. Generally used for bait.

GAME QUALITIES: Poor.

TACKLE: Pole or ultralight spinning.

BAITS AND LURES: Mostly a plankton feeder, it will take tiny pieces of cut squid or shrimp.

Pacific Kingcroaker

Menticihrrus elongatus

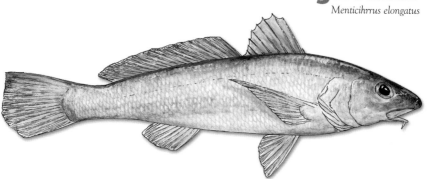

DESCRIPTION: Round nose and small mouth with single, rigid chin barbell. Sides are silvery and the back is light blue. Dorsal and anal fins are dusky. Upper lobe of tail fin is pointed, while lower lobe is round.

SIZE: Averages a pound or less. Maximum length is around 18 inches.

FOOD VALUE: Good.

GAME QUALITIES: Spirited fighter on light gear.

TACKLE: Light spinning or baitcasting; sometimes fly tackle.

BAITS AND LURES: Small crustaceans and marine worms work best. Small jigs bounced slowly on bottom may also draw strikes.

RANGE: *Baja California, Mexico, to Panama.*

WHERE TO FISH: *Usually caught in sandy surf, but also found in bays and river mouths.*

Queenfish

Seriphus politus

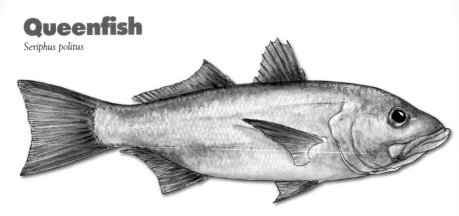

OTHER NAMES:

Kingfish

RANGE: *British Columbia, Canada, to southern Baja California, Mexico. Rare north of southern Oregon.*

WHERE TO FISH: *Schools are very common in summer around piers, dock pilings and tidal sloughs inshore. Moves to deeper water at night.*

DESCRIPTION: The mouth is very large and there is a distinctive wide gap between the first and second dorsal fins. Overall silvery with pale fins.

SIZE: Up to a foot or so; averages around 6-8 inches.

FOOD VALUE: Not much. Generally used for bait, live and cut.

GAME QUALITIES: Cooperative but small.

TACKLE: Sportsmen ignore them, except when they need bait. Children can take them on any tackle from poles to spinning gear.

BAITS AND LURES: Many baits produce. Cut shrimp, squid, fish and worms are popular ones.

Shortfin Corvina

Cynoscion parvipinnis

DESCRIPTION: The silvery color with bluish back is similar to several other Corvinas, but look for the very short pectoral fins, not extending to tips of pelvic fins. Inside of mouth is yellow, and canine teeth in the upper jaw are prominent.

SIZE: To about 7 pounds; averages 2-3 pounds. World record 6 pounds, 15 ounces.

FOOD VALUE: Excellent.

GAME QUALITIES: A strong fighter on light tackle.

TACKLE: Spinning and baitcasting; light ocean outfits.

BAITS AND LURES: Live small baitfish, spoons, sinking plugs, jigs.

OTHER NAMES:

Blue Corvina
Shortfin Seabass

RANGE: *Southern California (rare) to and including the Gulf of California, Mexico.*

WHERE TO FISH: *Surf, sand-bottom flats, shorelines, inshore channels and river mouths.*

Spotfin Croaker

Roncador stearnsi

OTHER NAMES:

Golden Croaker
Roncador

RANGE: *Southern California and west coast of Baja California, Mexico.*

WHERE TO FISH: *Can be found nearly anywhere along ocean or bay shorelines; an especially attractive surf and pier species. Also found in deeper water, up to about 50 feet.*

DESCRIPTION: A heavy-bodied Croaker with distinguishing black spot at base of pectoral fin. Color is dusky gray with lighter sides and belly. Sometimes has an overall brassy or golden hue. No barbel on chin.

SIZE: Most catches run 2-5 pounds, but a rare one will push 8 or 10 pounds. World record 3 pounds, 12 ounces.

FOOD VALUE: Very good.

GAME QUALITIES: A muscular and strong battler for its size.

TACKLE: Anything goes, but light spinning and baitcasting tackle provide the most sport.

BAITS AND LURES: Like most Croakers, feeds heavily on crustaceans and other invertebrates, but is not too reluctant to hit small lures worked slowly on the bottom.

Stolzmann's Corvina

Cynoscion stolzmanni

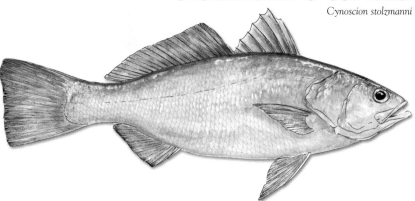

DESCRIPTION: Silver with steel-blue back. The fins are light gray and the tail is square. Pectoral fins are short, not extending to tips of pelvic fins. Large canine teeth in upper jaw.

SIZE: A large Corvina, it often weighs 15 to 25 pounds and can exceed 50 pounds.

FOOD VALUE: Very good.

GAME QUALITIES: Bigger ones are tough. Smaller ones put on a show but are landed fairly easily.

TACKLE: Spinning, baitcasting or light ocean gear.

BAITS AND LURES: Live baitfish and squid. Will also hit dead baits. Many are caught trolling, and also casting with jigs, spoons and swimming plugs. Lures generally work best when fished slowly near bottom.

OTHER NAMES:

Stolzmann's Weakfish

RANGE: Mexico to Panama.

WHERE TO FISH: Coastal areas, particularly estuaries and river and creek mouths. Also in surf and around rocky areas of shorelines.

Striped Corvina

Cynoscion reticulatus

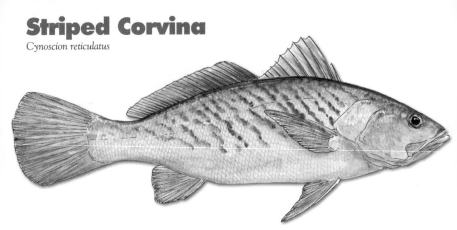

OTHER NAMES:

Striped Weakfish

RANGE: *Mexico to Panama.*

WHERE TO FISH: *Coastal areas around points and rocks. Plentiful in salty estuaries, but infrequently roams into brackish water.*

DESCRIPTION: Silver with brownish blotches along back and sides. Fins are yellow and the tail is rounded. Prominent canine teeth in upper jaw.

SIZE: A large Corvina, it averages perhaps 10-20 pounds and can exceed 50 pounds.

FOOD VALUE: Very good.

GAME QUALITIES: Showy and pretty tough, but without great stamina.

TACKLE: Spinning, baitcasting or light ocean gear.

BAITS AND LURES: Live baitfish are best, especially for big ones. Many are caught trolling off rocks and points, and also casting in estuaries with jigs, spoons and swimming plugs. Lures generally work best when fished slowly near bottom.

Totuava

Totoaba macdonaldi

DESCRIPTION: This largest of the Croakers has a blue back and silver-gray sides. Adults exhibit a brassy sheen overall. Fins are dusky, and the tail is convex. No barbels or canine teeth.

SIZE: Known to have reached 300 pounds, the few sport catches now made are mostly accidental, of fish weighing from 20 to perhaps 100 pounds.

FOOD VALUE: Excellent, but species is endangered and protected.

GAME QUALITIES: Very strong at all sizes.

TACKLE: Heavy spinning gear at a minimum. Light ocean tackle is the best.

BAITS AND LURES: Most of the rare catches are taken by trolling, usually with large plugs and spoons. Totuava also will take a wide variety of baitfish, plus shrimp and crabs.

OTHER NAMES:

**Machorro
Totoaba**

RANGE: Gulf of California, mostly northern portion.

WHERE TO FISH: Not targeted because of scarcity. Likes rocky points, deepwater dock areas and river mouths. Adults range farther offshore. The largest specimens are generally taken while fishing deep with live baits.

White Corvina

Cynoscion albus

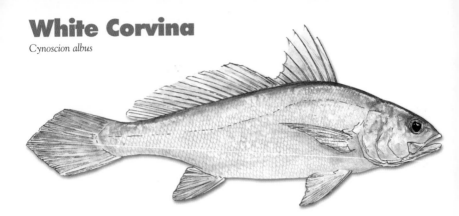

OTHER NAMES:

Whitefin Corvina
Whitefin Weakfish

RANGE: *Baja California, Mexico, to Panama.*

WHERE TO FISH: *Shoreline areas including surf, bays, estuaries and into brackish stretches of rivers.*

DESCRIPTION: Mostly silver with bluish-gray dorsal surface. Fins are white or transparent. The pectoral fins are long, reaching at least halfway to anal fin. Tail fin is arrow shaped.

SIZE: Most catches run 5-10 pounds; maximum is 30 pounds or more.

FOOD VALUE: Very good.

GAME QUALITIES: Not too strong, but showy and a hard striker.

TACKLE: Spinning and baitcasting outfits. Light ocean rigs for trolling.

BAITS AND LURES: Readily takes live fish and sometimes hits dead baits fished on bottom. Many are caught trolling, or casting with jigs, spoons and swimming plugs. Lures generally work best when fished slowly near bottom.

White Croaker

Genyonemus lineatus

DESCRIPTION: Color is silver, shading to dark gray above and yellowish on underside. Small chin barbells are barely noticeable. Black spot on pectoral fin. First ray of pelvic fin is threadlike and the fin also has a fleshy appendage at base.

SIZE: To 18 inches but usually less than a foot. World record 5 pounds, 3 ounces.

FOOD VALUE: Good.

GAME QUALITIES: Small but scrappy.

TACKLE: Sporty only on light spinning or baitcasting gear.

BAITS AND LURES: Pieces of shrimp, crab or squid. Seldom takes a lure.

OTHER NAMES:

Tomcod
Kingfish
Roncador

RANGE: *British Columbia (rarely) to Baja California, Mexico.*

WHERE TO FISH: *Often schools over sandy bottom near shore; also found in deeper water, to at least 200 feet.*

White Seabass

Atractoscion nobilis

OTHER NAMES:

California White Sea Bass
White Corvina
White Weakfish

RANGE: *Ranges as far north as Alaska, but is at its most plentiful, by far, from southern California southward to Baja and the Gulf of California, Mexico.*

WHERE TO FISH: *Numbers are depleted from past levels but with regulation, fishing is on the rebound. Look for White Seabass to be suspended around kelp beds and over rocky bottom. They always seem to be more plentiful where squid are numerous. Also found in the surf, especially smaller specimens.*

DESCRIPTION: Streamlined shape is silvery on the sides shading to metallic blue on the back. Fins are dusky, except the tail, which is yellow and square or concave. Dark spot on pectoral fin. Raised ridge on belly from pelvic fin to vent.

SIZE: Can push 100 pounds but most catches now run 10-25 pounds. World record 83 pounds, 12 ounces.

GAME QUALITIES: A good battler.

FOOD VALUE: Excellent.

TACKLE: Fairly heavy spinning and baitcasting outfits, along with light ocean gear and long livebait rods.

BAITS AND LURES: Squid is probably best, followed by Sardines and Anchovies. Best lures are metallic jigs, worked deep and slowly. Spoons, leadhead jigs and large plugs also produce. Lures should be worked at slow to medium speed.

Yellowfin Croaker

Umbrina roncador

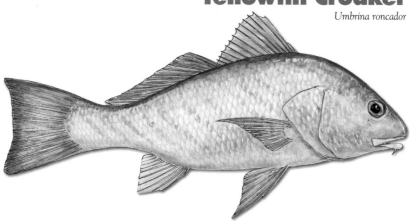

DESCRIPTION: Silvery with bluish back. Light brown or greenish oblique stripes onsides. Mouth is large and there is a single barbel under the chin.

SIZE: Averages 1 or 2 pounds but can exceed 5 pounds. World record 5 pounds, 8 ounces.

FOOD VALUE: Very good.

GAME QUALITIES: Large ones are strong on light gear.

TACKLE: Spinning is ideal, but light revolving-spool outfits are also good.

BAITS AND LURES: Shrimp, cut crab, or any sort of crustacean or mollusk. Also tiny jigs at times.

OTHER NAMES:

**Yellowfin Drum
Catalina Croaker**

RANGE: *Southern California to and including the Gulf of California, Mexico. Straggles to northern California.*

WHERE TO FISH: *Surf and shallow sandy areas of bays and river mouths.*

Just as human beings are right-handed or left-handed, flat-fishes are either right-eyed or left-eyed; that is, with the colored side up and the dorsal fin on top. That's easy to check, but trying to make rhyme or reason out of the common nomenclature is something else. The names Halibut, Flounder and Sole have no standard meanings and, in fact, "Sole" probably was originated by commercial fishermen to capitalize on the fame of the gourmet European dish, filet of sole. As for "Halibut," the giant Halibut of the northern sea is right-eyed, whereas the fish called California Halibut is usually left-eyed and frequently referred to as the California Flounder. The Turbot is just another of the right-eyed group, perhaps given its different name because it is proportionately thicker-bodied than other flatfishes of similar size. Despite their differences, the flat-fishes are much alike in being a treat on the table and popular targets of sport fishermen all along the coast. Although they spend much of their time on bottom, or even buried in mud and sand, most are aggressive predators that pursue baitfish—or a fisherman's lures—and strike savagely. How they rate as fighters depends directly on their size. Light tackle is sufficient for most of them but the Pacific Halibut can weigh hundreds of pounds and challenge even the heaviest sporting gear.

Bigmouth Sole

California Halibut

Pacific Sanddab

Butter Sole

C-O Sole

Diamond Turbot

Flathead Sole

Pacific Halibut

Petrale Sole

Rock Sole

Sand Sole

Starry Flounder

Bigmouth Sole

Hippoglossina stomata

RANGE: *Northern California to and including the Gulf of California, Mexico.*

WHERE TO FISH: *This is a deepwater species most often caught from partyboats at depths of 100 to 300 feet.*

DESCRIPTION: Left-eyed. Per its name, the mouth is large. Top is brown with blue dots and dark patches.

SIZE: Most run 12-15 inches.

FOOD VALUE: Excellent.

GAME QUALITIES: No battler but great eating.

TACKLE: Bottom-fishing gear.

LURES AND BAITS: Cut fish, cut squid, shrimp and other crustaceans.

California Halibut

Paralichthys californicus

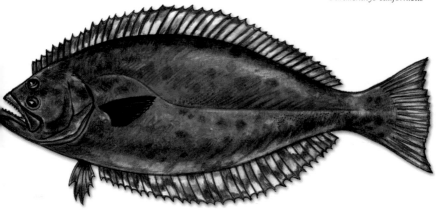

DESCRIPTION: Classed as left-eyed but, strangely, some specimens are right-eyed. Color is generally dark, with occasional mottling. The mouth is large and well equipped with sharp teeth. Careful! They can bite!

SIZE: Reported to 70 pounds or more but huge fish are now very rare and catches in the 5- to 10-pound class are good ones. World record 58 pounds, 9 ounces.

FOOD VALUE: Excellent.

GAME QUALITIES: Variable. Some are pretty docile while others fight like crazy. Regardless, all seem to resist violently upon being gaffed or pulled aboard a boat.

TACKLE: For inshore angling, long and fairly light rods are the norm, used with either spinning or casting reels. Not only are Halibut tricky to hook, but the hook pulls easily under too much pressure.

LURES AND BAITS: Many baits work well but Anchovies and other small baitfishes probably head the list, followed by squid. Baitfish work better when alive but are often productive dead or cut. Halibut also hit lures, such as plastic-tail or metallic jigs, quite well but whether natural or artificial, the offerings must be fished slowly and on bottom.

OTHER NAMES:

**California Flounder
Chicken Halibut
Southern Halibut**

RANGE: *Southern British Columbia to southern Baja California, Mexico.*

WHERE TO FISH: *Best prospects are in spring when fish are close to shore—often on sand flats just outside the surf and also in bays. They are also taken in deep water, up to about 300 feet.*

Pacific Sanddab

Citharichthys sordidus

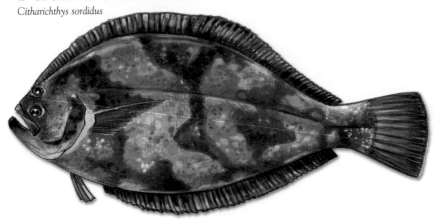

OTHER NAMES:

Mottled Sanddab
Lenguado

RANGE: Alaska to southern Baja California, Mexico.

WHERE TO FISH: Sandy bottom from about 30 feet out to far deeper water than hook-and-liners can reach.

DESCRIPTION: Left-eyed. Topside is brown or tan irregularly mottled with black and perhaps some orange spots. Dorsal, anal, and tail fins are black and the tail is round.

SIZE: Most are around a foot long. Maximum is perhaps 18 inches.

FOOD VALUE: Small fish but excellent taste.

GAME QUALITIES: Too small to pull much. The payoff is in the pan.

TACKLE: Any sort of bottom-fishing gear, the lighter the better.

LURES AND BAITS: Small baitfish, cut fish, cut squid, shrimp and other crustaceans.

Butter Sole

Pleuronectes isolepis

DESCRIPTION: Right-eyed. Topside is brown with dark brown and tan blotches, and sometimes yellow spots. Edges of the dorsal and anal fins are yellow.

SIZE: A foot or less.

FOOD VALUE: Excellent.

GAME QUALITIES: Poor because of size; sought mostly for table quality.

TACKLE: Light gear of the angler's choice.

LURES AND BAITS: Small Herrings and other baitfishes are good, as are shrimp. Occasionally hits small jigs worked slowly on bottom.

OTHER NAMES:

Scalyfin Flounder

RANGE: Alaska to southern California.

WHERE TO FISH: Shallow water on soft bottom in summer; more plentiful in northern sector of its range. Many caught in British Columbia.

C-O Sole

Pleuronichthys coenosus

OTHER NAMES:

C-O Turbot
Popeyed Turbot

RANGE: *Alaska to northern Baja California, Mexico.*

WHERE TO FISH: *Found over both sandy and rocky bottoms in fairly deep water, 50 feet to around 300 feet.*

DESCRIPTION: Right-eyed. The name derives from large dot-and-crescent marks on the tail, roughly simulating a "C" and "O". Also distinctive is a large, round, black spot in the center of the topside. Smaller dots or blotches also mark the brown body and the fins. The eyes are large and protruding.

SIZE: Averages a pound or 2; may reach 5 or more.

FOOD VALUE: Very good, but hide is tough to cut.

GAME QUALITIES: Mediocre.

TACKLE: Bottom-fishing gear, as light as can do the job.

LURES AND BAITS: Shellfish baits are best but small fish and cut fish are also taken.

Diamond Turbot

Hypsopsetta guttulata

DESCRIPTION: Right-eyed. Arching and peaked dorsal and anal fins give it its "diamond" shape. Top color is green or olive with blue dots. The mouth is small.

SIZE: To 18 inches, most under 12.

FOOD VALUE: Excellent.

GAME QUALITIES: So-so battle.

TACKLE: An unusual catch, seldom targeted, so any sort of light-line gear will do.

LURES AND BAITS: Only shellfish baits are apt to produce: clams, shrimp, squid.

RANGE: Northern California to southern Baja California, Mexico.

WHERE TO FISH: Mostly shallow, muddy or sandy water of shorelines and bays, although some are taken in depths up to 150 feet.

Flathead Sole

Hippoglossoides elassodon

RANGE: *Alaska to central California.*

WHERE TO FISH: *They like soft bottom but have a wide variance in depth, from near shore to more than 1,000 feet. They're caught most often, however, in around 100 feet.*

DESCRIPTION: Right-eyed and very thin. Topside is usually dark brown blotched with lighter brown. Upper jaw has only one row of teeth.

SIZE: Averages 2-3 pounds.

FOOD VALUE: Excellent.

GAME QUALITIES: Not a great battler.

TACKLE: Bottom-fishing gear offshore. Reasonably light casting or spinning gear inshore.

LURES AND BAITS: Although shellfish and marine worms are its usual prey, it will take nearly any fish or shellfish bait, plus jigs bounced on bottom.

Pacific Halibut

Hippoglossus stenolepis

DESCRIPTION: Right-eyed, although a rare specimen is left-eyed. Size alone usually is enough of an identifier. The topside is dark brown to nearly black and may have spots or blotches. The mouth is proportionately small—not extending past the eye—but is still huge because of the overall size. The tail is slightly concave.

SIZE: Wow! It's not awfully uncommon at 200 pounds and has been reported to reach as much as 800 pounds! Most catches probably fall in the 10- to 50-pound class. World record 459 pounds.

FOOD VALUE: Very good.

GAME QUALITIES: A strong and stubborn fighter that uses its muscle and flat sides to best advantage. It also is a roughhouse foe on the gaff or in the boat.

TACKLE: Just as Halibut come in all sizes, so does the tackle used for them. Since giant fish are always a possibility, ocean outfits with 50-pound or heavier lines are routinely used and certainly with good reason, but there is a growing trend toward light-tackle fishing.

LURES AND BAITS: Halibut feed on just about everything down there—small fish, crabs, clams, squids, whatever. All those are good baits. Artificial lures are often accepted just as eagerly. Casters prefer heavy metallic or hair jigs, which they bounce on the bottom. Fly fishermen score with sinking lines. Halibut are also caught by trolling with Salmon tackle.

OTHER NAMES:

**Giant Halibut
Northern Halibut
Right Halibut
Alabato**

RANGE: *Alaska to northern Baja California, Mexico, but much more common in the northern portions of its range.*

WHERE TO FISH: *Alaskan (and Canadian) waters are the best hunting grounds for Halibut, especially the overgrown specimens. Small fish stick pretty much to inshore waters, say 20 or 30 feet. The big ones hug the continental shelf at depths up to 3,000 feet most of the year, but also go shallow in the warmer seasons, and can be found during the summer in water ranging from about 30 to 500 feet.*

Petrale Sole

Eopsetta jordani

OTHER NAMES:

**Brill
Roundnose
Flounder**

RANGE: *Alaska to northern Baja California, Mexico.*

WHERE TO FISH: *Usually caught from deep water in mixed bags with Rockfish and others, but it does roam close to shore during warmer weather. Like most Flatfishes, it likes soft bottom, especially if it's close to rocks or other structure.*

DESCRIPTION: Right-eyed. Top is uniform light brown, with dark patches on the dorsal and anal fins. The mouth is large, with small teeth in the upper jaw.

SIZE: Averages 2 or 3 pounds; occasionally reaches 6 or 7 pounds.

FOOD VALUE: Excellent. Many consider it tops.

GAME QUALITIES: Fair. It's a lightweight and generally is caught on overpowering tackle.

TACKLE: Bottom-fishing gear offshore. Reasonably light casting or spinning gear inshore.

LURES AND BAITS: A democratic feeder, it will take nearly any fish or shellfish bait, plus jigs bounced on bottom.

Rock Sole

Pleuronectes bilineatus

DESCRIPTION: Right-eyed. Basic color of the top side is brown with numerous dots on both body and fins. Dots range from white to yellow to red. Like many flatfish, this fellow is adept at changing color for camouflage.

SIZE: A nice-size flattie, it can grow to as much as 2 feet, but the average is 12-14 inches.

FOOD VALUE: Excellent.

GAME QUALITIES: Mediocre.

TACKLE: Light gear will do inshore but many are caught on heavy bottom-fishing tackle.

LURES AND BAITS: Not overly picky about bait, it will take crabs, shrimp, marine worms and whole small baitfish or cut fish. Catches on lures are possible but not common.

OTHER NAMES:

Broadfin Flounder Roughback Sole

RANGE: Alaska to southern California; more numerous in its northern sector.

WHERE TO FISH: Comes into shallow water during summer but most are caught deep, in potluck fishing from party boats or private craft. Likes sandy or gravel bottom.

Sand Sole

Psettichthys melanostictus

OTHER NAMES:

Fringe Flounder

RANGE: *Alaska to southern California.*

WHERE TO FISH: *Quite common in sandy areas near shore, including quiet surf of coves and bays. Often taken by pier and shore anglers.*

DESCRIPTION: Right-eyed. Top varies from light tan to brown, according to background, and has many small black spots. Several forward rays of the dorsal fin are elongated, giving a crest-like effect.

SIZE: Usual catches run 1-3 pounds, although fish over 5 pounds are sometimes taken.

FOOD VALUE: Very good.

GAME QUALITIES: Not bad on very light tackle.

TACKLE: Spinning will provide the most sport.

LURES AND BAITS: Takes many natural baits including shrimp, squid, clams, worms and cut fish. Small jigs can also produce some strikes.

Starry Flounder

Platichthys stellatus

DESCRIPTION: Right-eyed. Top of body is very dark. Dorsal and anal fins are arched and pointed and marked with several orange or reddish bars with white spaces in between. The skin is very rough.

SIZE: Most fall in the 1- to 5-pound range but some surpass 10 pounds. World record 3 pounds, 12 ounces.

FOOD VALUE: Good but not as highly regarded as some other flatties.

GAME QUALITIES: Fun on light line.

TACKLE: Spinning provides best sport, but light revolving-reel gear is highly productive too.

LURES AND BAITS: Shrimp, crabs and marine worms do best among naturals. Many are taken on jigs bounced along the bottom.

OTHER NAMES:

Rough Jacket

RANGE: Alaska to southern California; more plentiful in colder waters.

WHERE TO FISH: Plentiful in inshore waters, including bays, estuaries and river mouths over most of its range. Likes sandy or gravel bottom.

As noted in the preceding chapter, sorting out the common names of flatfishes is something of a problem, but it's a snap compared to pinning down the identification of the many species of fish that long have been called Trouts, Salmons and Chars. For one thing, while at sea they are all much alike in superficial coloration, being mostly silver before gaining the vivid colors that bedeck most of them after they spend some time in fresh water. Moreover, just separating the Trouts from the Salmons from the Chars is no easy task in itself, because popular names have long been arbitrary and confusing. For instance, the Steelhead and Cutthroat "Trouts" are scientifically classified as Salmons, and the Dolly Varden as a Char; therefore, no "real" Trout at all inhabit Pacific coastal waters. Scientists avoid such confusion by referring to all members of the family as Salmonids. Certain physical characteristics of each species are more reliable identifiers than color, and these are noted in the descriptions that follow. Regardless of classification, however, all Salmonids, regardless of their common names, are game fish of the very highest stature, and this is particularly true when they are hooked at sea or in tidewater, for then they are at their physical peak and well prepared for a good fight.

Salmons, Chars and "Trouts"

Arctic Char

Chinook Salmon

Chum Salmon

Coho Salmon

Cutthroat Trout

Dolly Varden

Pink Salmon

Sockeye Salmon

Steelhead

Arctic Char

Salvelinus alpinus

OTHER NAMES:

Blueback Char
Quebec Red Trout
White Trout
Sunapee

RANGE: *Alaska and sub-Arctic Canada.*

WHERE TO FISH: *Sea-run Char are fishable from shore in river mouths and estuaries of the far North.*

DESCRIPTION: Although their colors turn bright after they ascend coastal streams, Arctic Char in the ocean and estuaries are usually solid silver on the sides, with gray to blue backs. Pale whitish or pinkish dots can sometimes be seen. Fins are yellowish and the tail is slightly forked.

SIZE: Sea-run Char often weigh 5-10 pounds, although 2- or 3-pounders are more common. The potential is to more than 25 pounds.

FOOD VALUE: Very good when taken in salt water or lower reaches of streams.

GAME QUALITIES: Sea-run fish strike hard and are strong fighters, but they jump infrequently.

TACKLE: Char feed on small baitfish, so spinning and light baitcasting gear are the best tackle choices. Fly fishing can sometimes produce but Char make better fly targets after they reach fresh water.

LURES AND BAITS: Flashy spoons and spinners are by far the best lures. Minnow-imitating streamers should be chosen for fly fishing.

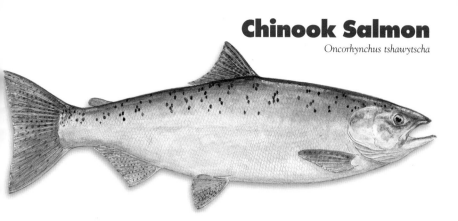

Chinook Salmon

Oncorhynchus tshawytscha

DESCRIPTION: At sea the Chinook is basically silver in color, shading to blue or blue-green on the upper sides and darker blue on the back. It is profusely spotted above the lateral line, on the dorsal fin, and on both lobes of the tail fin. Breeding fish are darker in color, often green or purplish. Kings are distinguishable from other Salmons of similar size and appearance by the black gums at the base of the teeth.

SIZE: Largest of the Salmons, adult Chinook weighing from 5 to 20 pounds are common catches, while 40- and 50-pounders are not too unusual. World record 97 pounds, 4 ounces.

FOOD VALUE: Top of the heap, fresh or smoked.

GAME QUALITIES: King Salmon are not the best acrobats, but are always formidable foes.

TACKLE: Long rods are the standard, but reel preferences vary widely from spinning to baitcasting to light ocean models. Another popular outfit is a long fly rod with a large, single action reel. Any of that gear is used for trolling with downriggers or heavy weights, and also for mooching with sinkers and natural bait. Fly tackle is mostly reserved for upstream waters.

LURES AND BAITS: The vast majority of Kings are taken either on deep-trolled lures or on live and cut baits, mainly Herring and Candlefish. Bright dodgers rigged ahead of the lures add to the strikes. Metallic lures up to several ounces are used for deep jigging. Casters in the rivers rely mostly on spoons and spinners.

OTHER NAMES:

King Salmon
Spring Salmon
Tyee
Quinnat
Blackmouth

RANGE: From Alaska to central California, straggling to southern California.

WHERE TO FISH: Anglers concentrate their efforts either in deep water of bays and estuaries where the fish gather for their spawning runs from late spring to early fall or else well offshore around rips and upwellings. They are also heavily fished in the lower reaches of the spawning rivers.

Chum Salmon

Oncorhynchus keta

OTHER NAMES:

Dog Salmon
Calico Salmon
Fall Salmon

RANGE: *Arctic Alaska to Oregon, straggling to southern California.*

WHERE TO FISH: *Seldom targeted, Chums are usually taken incidentally to fishing for other Salmon species.*

DESCRIPTION: Shiny blue-green on top with tiny speckles but no distinct spots. The tail is edged in black. In fresh water the males develop bars of purple or green. Those colors are less vivid on females, which also have a dark streak, along the lateral line. Breeding males have large teeth, and these, plus the pronounced hooked snout, account for the name Dog Salmon.

SIZE: Chums average 4-10 pounds but fish of 25 pounds are fairly common and the top size is near 30. World record 35 pounds.

FOOD VALUE: Good but less highly ranked than other Salmons. Fine smoked.

GAME QUALITIES: A strong and determined fighter but not very showy.

TACKLE: Light spinning and fly gear.

LURES AND BAITS: Streamer flies and shrimp flies; spinners and small spoons also do well. Chums are usually picky biters.

Coho Salmon

Oncorhynchus kisutch

DESCRIPTION: The Coho is less liberally spotted than the King Salmon, and only the lower lobe of the caudal fin is spotted. Coloration is silver with bluish back and white underparts. The Coho is easily distinguished from the Chinook by its gums, which are white. Breeding fish in the rivers grow darker in color, with olive back and red sides.

SIZE: Usually weighs in the range of 2 to 6 pounds in early season with larger fish, up to around 10 pounds, available in the fall. Top potential is 20 pounds or so. World record 33 pounds, 4 ounces.

FOOD VALUE: Excellent fresh or smoked.

GAME QUALITIES: A strong and speedy fighter that often jumps in stirring fashion.

TACKLE: For trolling, spinning gear is popular, as are large level-wind reels and single-action reels, all usually with long rods. Coho often school and feed at the surface, making exciting casting targets with light spinning and fly tackle. The same kinds of light tackle are used in river fishing.

LURES AND BAITS: As for King Salmon, a great deal of fishing is done with large spoons, plugs, plastic squids and whole baitfish or rigged fillets. Trolling probably heads the list of approaches, although mooching and drifting with live or cut baitfish is close in popularity in many areas. Live forage includes Herring, Candlefish and Sardines. Metallic lures and shiny streamer flies are the ticket for spin and fly casting.

OTHER NAMES:

**Silver Salmon
Medium Red
Salmon
Blueback**

RANGE: *Major range is from Point Hope, Alaska, to central California. Straggles to northern Mexico.*

WHERE TO FISH: *From bays and river mouths to far offshore, wherever bait is concentrated. Usually sticks fairly near the surface.*

Cutthroat Trout

Oncorhynchus clarki

OTHER NAMES:

Blackspotted Trout Mountain Trout

RANGE: *Common from the Eel River in northern California to Alaska's Prince William Sound.*

WHERE TO FISH: *Lower reaches of streams, plus shorelines of bays and estuaries.*

DESCRIPTION: Color is silvery with olive or bluish back. Similar in appearance to the Steelhead but has more spots and also sports the distinctive red "cutthroat" slash around the jaw or gills.

SIZE: Big fish, topping 6 pounds, are mostly interior residents. Sea-run fish average perhaps 1-2 pounds with an occasional 5-pounder reported and bigger ones always possible. World record, 41 pounds.

FOOD VALUE: Excellent.

GAME QUALITIES: Outstanding for its size.

TACKLE: Light spinning gear is ideal, but fly outfits can be used to great effect in many Cutthroat waters along the coast.

LURES AND BAITS: Spin casters rely on small spoons and spinners, the latter often fished ahead of a small natural bait, such as minnow, bait plug or earthworm. Numerous patterns of streamer flies are used but brightly colored ones probably lead the pack.

Dolly Varden

Salvelinus malma

DESCRIPTION: In sea-run adults the sides are silver to white, while the back, upper head and upper sides are dark blue. Similar in appearance to the sea-run Char, it is distinguishable by counting the gill rakers. The Dolly sports a maximum of 21 while the Char has 23 or more.

SIZE: Most estuarine catches run 2-5 pounds. Potential is to nearly 20 pounds.

FOOD VALUE: Good.

GAME QUALITIES: Strong but not very acrobatic.

TACKLE: Spinning gear or any Salmon tackle.

LURES AND BAITS: Best lures are trolled spoons, spinners and flies. Small baitfish and cut plugs are productive natural baits.

OTHER NAMES:

Dolly Varden Trout

RANGE: *Arctic and Pacific drainages from Alaska to Puget Sound. Landlocked fish are found farther south as well. World record, 19 pounds, 4 ounces.*

WHERE TO FISH: *Estuaries and lower reaches of rivers.*

Pink Salmon

Oncorhynchus gorbuscha

OTHER NAMES:

Humpback Salmon
Humpy

RANGE: *Alaska to northern California. Most plentiful from Puget Sound northward.*

WHERE TO FISH: *Rip currents in bays and offshore draw both Pinks and Coho, but the latter are usually the preferred targets.*

DESCRIPTION: While in salt water, Pink Salmon are metallic blue on top, with silver sides. Black spots, bolder than those on the Chinook, are liberally sprinkled on the back and entire tail. In the rivers, spawning fish quickly develop the characteristic hump. Males turn dark brown with white underside. Females are dusky green and patchy.

SIZE: Smallest of the Salmons, most Pinks weigh 3 or 4 pounds, with an occasional catch to about 10 pounds. World record 14 pounds, 7 ounces.

FOOD VALUE: Fine eating but less highly regarded than the Coho and Chinook.

GAME QUALITIES: Outstanding gamester and good jumper; rather small average size dictates light lines.

TACKLE: Any sort of Salmon tackle, but the lighter the better. Sometimes fly gear is productive when fish are surfacing.

LURES AND BAITS: Pinks eagerly hit trolled plugs, squids and spoons, and also drifted or mooched natural baits, especially cut Herring. They also take a caster's spoons and jigs, as well as streamer flies.

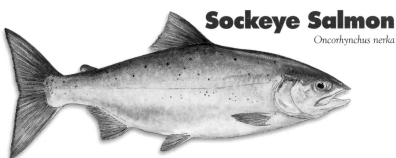

Sockeye Salmon

Oncorhynchus nerka

DESCRIPTION: Bright silvery sides with bluish back and tiny black dots on back and tail fin. During upstream runs color changes to the "Red Salmon" phase, in which males have bright red bodies, green heads. Female's colors similar but duller.

SIZE: Usually from around 4 to 8 pounds; occasionally as much as 15 pounds. World record 15 pounds, 3 ounces.

FOOD VALUE: Rich, red flesh, perhaps best of all salmons.

GAME QUALITIES: Good fighter, much like the Coho.

TACKLE: Spinning and mooching gear.

LURES AND BAITS: Spinners and small spoons work best, with bright skirted lures for trolling.

OTHER NAMES:

Red Salmon
Blueback

RANGE: *Alaska to Oregon, straggling to southern California.*

WHERE TO FISH: *Most are caught in the rivers, but they can be taken along the coast and in bays by fishing deep. A commercial standby, it is not as popular among anglers.*

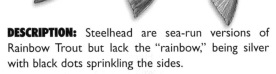

Steelhead

Oncorhynchus mykiss

DESCRIPTION: Steelhead are sea-run versions of Rainbow Trout but lack the "rainbow," being silver with black dots sprinkling the sides.

SIZE: Runs of small Steelhead, about 2 or 3 pounds, provide much sport in bay areas during spring and summer. In fall runs, 10- to 15-pounders are common. World record 42 pounds, 2 ounces.

FOOD VALUE: Excellent.

GAME QUALITIES: None better. Many fly fishermen consider it equal to the Atlantic Salmon.

TACKLE: Salmon tackle is ideal but light gear is used.

LURES AND BAITS: Steelhead hit a variety of spinners and spoons.

OTHER NAMES:

Rainbow
Steelie

RANGE: *Estuaries and rivers from about the middle of California to Alaska.*

WHERE TO FISH: *Although "classic" Steelhead fishing takes place inland, many are taken in bays and river mouths.*

Also known as Seaperches, the Surfperches are a staple catch not only of surf and shore fishermen but of boating anglers who work near the coastline and in bays. There are around two dozen species, of which the best known and largest are included here. At one time, the various types were conversationally separated by referring to some as Seaperch, others as Surfperch, and still others simply as Perch. Nowadays, however, it is far more common to hear them all called Surfperch. While they cannot be classed as great gamesters, they provide loads of fun for fishermen of all ages because they usually are willing biters and make great fish dinners. When in the surf, these fish are more likely to be foraging not far from the angler's feet than a long cast away. That means they can easily be caught with unsophisticated tackle, as well as with baits gathered from or near the beach. Many Surfperch of various species are also taken from jetties, piers and shoreside rocks.

Chapter

The Surfperches

Barred Surfperch

Black Perch

Calico Surfperch

Rainbow Surfperch

Redtail Surfperch

Rubberlip Seaperch

Shiner Perch

Silver Surfperch

Striped Surfperch

Walleye Surfperch

White Seaperch

Barred Surfperch

Amphistichus argenteus

RANGE: *Northern California to northern Baja California, Mexico.*

WHERE TO FISH: *In addition to the surf, they are caught near rocks or pilings and from piers.*

DESCRIPTION: Back and upper sides are brown to olive; lower sides and belly silver. Several reddish-brown vertical bars mark the sides, with scattered dots in between. Fins are light, edged with black.

SIZE: Averages between a half-pound and 2 pounds; rarely reaches about 4 pounds. World record 4 pounds, 2 ounces.

FOOD VALUE: Good.

GAME QUALITIES: Spunky on light tackle.

TACKLE: Spinning, baitcasting and light surf outfits.

LURES AND BAITS: Natural bait is a must. Sand crabs are probably best, but they will also bite shrimp and nearly any sort of small or cut shellfish bait.

Black Perch

Embiotoca jacksoni

DESCRIPTION: The overall color varies from dark gray to brown or reddish, with faint vertical bars. Black margin around upper mouth.

SIZE: From less than a pound to about 3 pounds.

FOOD VALUE: Good.

GAME QUALITIES: Tough for its size.

TACKLE: Light spinning and baitcasting; sometimes poles.

LURES AND BAITS: Shrimp, crab or pieces of clams, worms or mussels.

OTHER NAMES:

Black Surfperch
Butterlips

RANGE: *Northern California to central Baja California, Mexico.*

WHERE TO FISH: *Unlike most other Surfperches, it is not often found in the surf, preferring rocky areas near kelp. It also enters bays and can be found around pilings and piers.*

Calico Surfperch

Amphistichus koelzi

RANGE: *Washington to northern Baja California. Most common in California south of San Francisco.*

WHERE TO FISH: *Surf.*

DESCRIPTION: Overall color looks silvery, perhaps with goldish sheen. The back is gray-blue to olive and the fins are light red. The head and lower forward part of the body are also red-tinted. Small brown spots on the side form thin vertical bars.

SIZE: A 1-pounder is a big one.

FOOD VALUE: A tasty panfish.

GAME QUALITIES: Spirited fight without much muscle.

TACKLE: Light spinning, baitcasting and surf gear.

LURES AND BAITS: Bits of shrimp, crab and other shellfish.

Rainbow Surfperch

Hypsurus caryi

DESCRIPTION: Rainbow is right! Red or orange bars descend from the back, while blue or red stripes mark the sides. Blue also dots the head. Dorsal and anal fins wear black blotches.

SIZE: Fish over 1 pound are good ones, but a rare specimen will hit 2 pounds.

FOOD VALUE: Good.

GAME QUALITIES: Scrappy for its size.

TACKLE: Light gear—spinning, baitcasting, surf outfits.

LURES AND BAITS: Crabs and other shellfish baits are a must.

OTHER NAMES:

Rainbow Seaperch

RANGE: *Northern California, to northern Baja California, Mexico.*

WHERE TO FISH: *This one is not a surf dweller, although it's often found over sandy bottom. Most are caught around shoreline rocks, especially close to kelp beds.*

Redtail Surfperch

Amphistichus rhodoterus

OTHER NAMES:

Pinkfish

RANGE: *A very popular catch from central California all the way into Canada.*

WHERE TO FISH: *Primarily the sandy surf, but it roams into bays as well.*

DESCRIPTION: The namesake tail is indeed usually red, as are the other fins, although it might range from pink to maroon. The sides are silvery, marked with several reddish vertical bars.

SIZE: Most run 1-2 pounds with 3-pounders fairly common. May top 4 pounds on rare occasion.

FOOD VALUE: Very good.

GAME QUALITIES: Scrappy for its size.

TACKLE: Light spinning, baitcasting and surf gear.

LURES AND BAITS: Crabs or cut crab, marine worms, shrimp, clams, mussels.

Rubberlip Seaperch

Rhacochilus toxotes

DESCRIPTION: Overall color can range from silvery to dark gray with darker bars on the side. Main giveaway are the lips, which are very thick—noticeably larger than other Surfperches—and white or pinkish in color.

SIZE: This is the largest Surfperch, averaging 2 pounds or so and sometimes reaching 4 or more.

FOOD VALUE: Very good.

GAME QUALITIES: Tough battler; uses its side for extra resistance.

TACKLE: Stout spinning or baitcasting gear or light ocean tackle.

LURES AND BAITS: Crab, squid and shrimp are all very productive.

RANGE: Northern California to central Baja California, Mexico.

WHERE TO FISH: Skip the surf and try rocky shorelines, piers or docks; also rocky areas offshore around kelp beds. Often caught in 100 feet or water or slightly more.

Shiner Perch

Cymatogaster aggregata

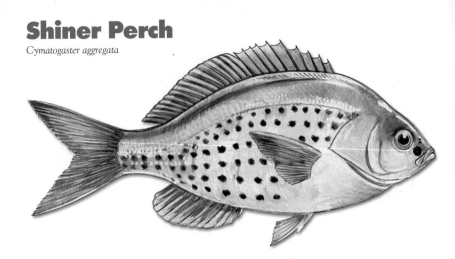

OTHER NAMES:

Shiner

RANGE: *Alaska to northern Baja California, Mexico.*

WHERE TO FISH: *Probably the most plentiful Surfperch everywhere along the Pacific Coast, it is found in all shallow nearshore habitats and in bays. Very common around many piers and other shore-fishing spots.*

DESCRIPTION: Color is silvery with an olive back. Black dots form about eight longitudinal stripes, which are often interrupted by three yellow, vertical bands. Breeding males are very dark overall.

SIZE: A few inches.

FOOD VALUE: A tasty panfish but watch out for the bones.

GAME QUALITIES: Not much.

TACKLE: It's a favorite of children but shunned by most anglers. Any light gear, usually pole or spinning, will do.

LURES AND BAITS: Bits of shrimp, crab or other shellfish.

Silver Surfperch

Hyperprosopon ellipticum

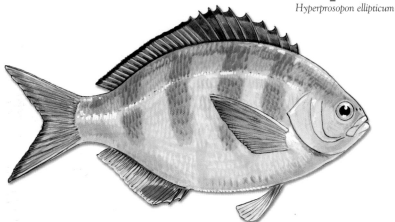

DESCRIPTION: Color is silvery gray or green above, lighter below. Faint bars of yellow or pink on sides. Tail is reddish, edged in black, and the eye is large.

SIZE: Averages a few ounces in weight; seldom as much as 1 pound.

FOOD VALUE: Good panfish.

GAME QUALITIES: Not much.

TACKLE: Here's another little fellow that's a favorite of the younger set, who mostly use poles or light spinning gear.

LURES AND BAITS: Bits of shrimp or other shellfish.

RANGE: *British Columbia, Canada, to northern Baja California, Mexico.*

WHERE TO FISH: *Found in both sandy surf and around piers, rocks and other structure. Also in bays.*

Striped Surfperch

Embiotoca lateralis

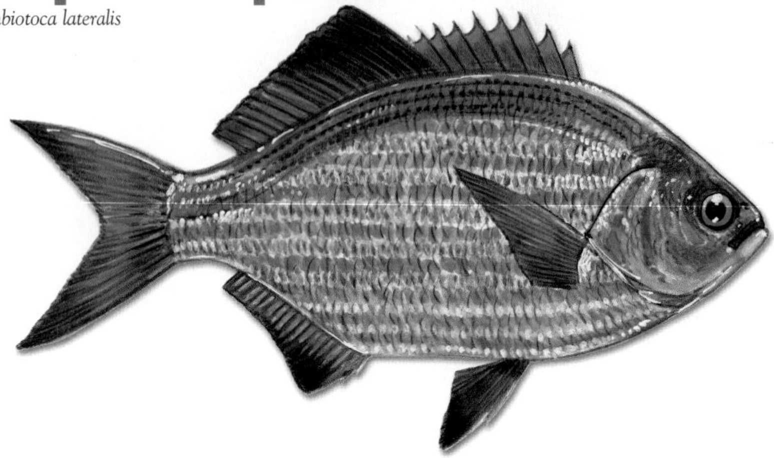

OTHER NAMES:

Seaperch

RANGE: *Alaska to northern Baja California, Mexico.*

WHERE TO FISH: *Less in surf than along rocky shoreline areas of both coast and bays. If in surf, usually is close to rocks.*

DESCRIPTION: A brilliant fellow with horizontal stripes of blue and red over a coppery background. Blue streaks mark the head and gill cover.

SIZE: Averages a pound or 2; seldom larger.

FOOD VALUE: Good.

GAME QUALITIES: A scrappy foe on light line.

TACKLE: Light spinning or baitcasting gear, or pole.

LURES AND BAITS: Crabs or pieces of other shellfish, such as marine worms or mussels.

Walleye Surfperch
Hyperprosopon argenteum

DESCRIPTION: Large round eye and very deep body mark this fellow, whose overall color is dark blue on top with silvery sides and belly. Small fish often show narrow yellow bars. Tips of the pectoral fins are black, as is the trailing edge of the tail.

SIZE: Frequently weighs a pound, sometimes 2.

FOOD VALUE: Good.

GAME QUALITIES: A spunky lightweight.

TACKLE: Light surf gear, spinning, baitcasting.

LURES AND BAITS: Sand crabs or any small crab, plus shrimp, marine worms and clams.

RANGE: British Columbia, Canada, to central Baja California, Mexico.

WHERE TO FISH: This is a surf favorite all along the coast, although the best spots often are near rocks.

White Seaperch
Phanerodon furcatus

DESCRIPTION: The back is greenish and the sides are silvery, but with a distinctive dark line at the base of the dorsal fin. The edges of the anal and caudal fins also are dark.

SIZE: One pound is a good average; seldom grows much larger.

FOOD VALUE: Good.

GAME QUALITIES: Scrappy for its size.

TACKLE: Anything light.

LURES AND BAITS: Crabs and other crustaceans are best.

RANGE: Southern British Columbia, Canada, to northern Baja California, Mexico.

WHERE TO FISH: Prefers calmer water than the surf. Common around piers and docks and on soft bottom near rocks.

Members of this huge and widespread family are often called "Rock Cod" but, in reality, they belong to the Scorpionfish family, not the Cod clan. Of the more than 60 species, the two dozen or so included here are common and popular catches. As a group, they constitute one of the richest and most reliable resources for bottom-fishermen from Alaska to southern California. While they are mainstays of off-shore partyboats all along the coast, many kinds are equally available to folks fishing in shallow water, even from shore and inside bays. Although some types are brightly colored, few will ever win any prizes for beauty, but they have other attributes that make them very attractive in the eyes of anglers. Not the least of these is their perpetually large appetites, backed by big mouths that eagerly ingest a great variety of baits and lures. Additionally, most of them reward the successful fisherman with delicious fillets. A word of caution: All Rockfish have sharp dorsal spines that can administer a painful and slightly poisonous wound, so they should be handled with great care. Only a stab from the California Scorpionfish, however, is likely to cause really intense pain.

Chapter

The Rockfishes

Black-and-Yellow Rockfish

Black Rockfish

Blue Rockfish

Bocaccio

Brown Rockfish

California Scorpionfish

Canary Rockfish

Chilipepper

China Rockfish

Copper Rockfish

Cowcod

Grass Rockfish

Greenspotted Rockfish

Kelp Rockfish

Olive Rockfish

Quillback Rockfish

Redbanded Rockfish

Redstripe Rockfish

Rosy Rockfish

Silvergray Rockfish

Speckled Rockfish

Tiger Rockfish

Vermilion Rockfish

Widow Rockfish

Yelloweye Rockfish

Yellowtail Rockfish

Black-and-Yellow Rockfish

Sebastes chrysomelas

RANGE: *Northern California to Baja California, Mexico.*

WHERE TO FISH: *Close inshore around rocks, points and kelp. This Rockfish generally sticks to water less than 50 feet deep or so.*

DESCRIPTION: Deep olive-brown to black, with several yellow blotches on the back and upper sides.

SIZE: Most 1-2 pounds. Maximum 16 inches.

FOOD VALUE: Very good.

GAME QUALITIES: Not bad on light tackle.

TACKLE: Spinning or baitcasting gear.

LURES AND BAITS: Small jigs and spoons take plenty. Cut baits from fish or shellfish take more.

Black Rockfish

Sebastes melanops

DESCRIPTION: Overall color is black or blue-black mottled with gray. Belly is dingy white. Some specimens show a gray stripe.

SIZE: Averages 2-4 pounds; reaches at least 10 pounds. World record 10 pounds.

FOOD VALUE: Good.

GAME QUALITIES: Among the best of its clan. It strikes hard and runs with strength and spirit, if not for long distance.

TACKLE: Gear can be as varied as the situations in which these fish are found. Light spinning and baitcasting outfits, or even fly tackle, is perfectly at home when they are encountered on top. And because they aren't necessarily bottom huggers, many are caught on Salmon-trolling rigs in the Northwest and Canada. On the other side of the coin, however, they are partyboat favorites and huge numbers are hauled up with bottom-fishing outfits.

LURES AND BAITS: A great many Salmon and Bass lures will take mid-depth or surfacing fish, including topwater plugs and streamer flies. Spoons and plastic-tail jigs are among the favorites. Like other Rockfish, they are not particularly choosy about natural baits, although sometimes more inclined to go for live small baitfish.

OTHER NAMES:

Sea Bass
Black Sea Bass

RANGE: *Alaska to northern California.*

WHERE TO FISH: *This is one of the most widely foraging Rockfish, often roaming open water—even at the surface—as well as hugging the bottom on reefs. Its range of depth is also wide. Many are caught close inshore, while others are found as deep as 1,000 feet or more. Even when the water is 300-500 feet deep, schools of these "Bass" may be feeding on or near the surface.*

Blue Rockfish

Sebastes mystinus

OTHER NAMES:

Sea Bass

RANGE: *Alaska to central California.*

WHERE TO FISH: *Often encountered near the surface or off the bottom, they prefer shallow reef areas, but also forage around kelp and over deep reefs.*

DESCRIPTION: Almost a dead ringer for the Black Sea Bass, the Blue has a smaller mouth and usually is bluer in color. The two species often hang out together.

SIZE: Averages 2-4 pounds; occasionally to 10 pounds. World record 8 pounds, 6 ounces.

FOOD VALUE: Good.

GAME QUALITIES: Hard fighter on light line.

TACKLE: Light outfits, or even fly tackle.

LURES AND BAITS: A great many lures will take surfacing fish, including topwater plugs and streamer flies. They will hit all the popular natural baits.

Bocaccio

Sebastes paucispinis

OTHER NAMES:

Snapper
Salmon Grouper

RANGE: *Alaska to central Baja California, Mexico.*

WHERE TO FISH: *Ranges widely from about 90 feet out to 1,000 feet. Although it orients to rocky structure in the manner of other Rockfishes, it also can be found on mud or sand bottom.*

DESCRIPTION: Leaner than most Rockfish, this one is brownish or red above; pink or shiny red on the sides. The mouth is large and there is a dip in head.

SIZE: A good-size Rockfish, it often reaches 10 pounds or more and can exceed 20 pounds.

FOOD VALUE: Very good.

GAME QUALITIES: One of the best of its clan for fight.

TACKLE: Usually, bottom-fishing tackle gets the nod.

LURES AND BAITS: Live baitfish are superior, although cut baits and metallic jigs take many fish.

Brown Rockfish

Sebastes auriculatus

DESCRIPTION: Light brown, mottled with shades of darker brown. Dark bars often appear on the back. Fins are pink.

SIZE: Most run 1-3 pounds. Common to about 6 pounds and can exceed 10.

FOOD VALUE: Very good.

GAME QUALITIES: Tough on light gear.

TACKLE: Spinning and baitcasting are fine for inshore use. Stout boat tackle is needed offshore.

LURES AND BAITS: Rock Cod will inhale virtually any popular natural bait of appropriate size.

OTHER NAMES:

Rock Cod

RANGE: *Alaska to Baja California, Mexico. Most heavily fished from central California northward.*

WHERE TO FISH: *Shallow water is best, around rocks, kelp and pilings or other structure. Some are taken from reefs and rocks up to 300 feet deep.*

California Scorpionfish

Scorpaena guttata

DESCRIPTION: Color can change drastically according to environment, ranging from brilliant red to dull gray or brown, with darker blotches present in all phases. Dorsal spines are sharp and venomous enough to cause great pain. Pectorals are fan-like.

SIZE: Most are 8-12 inches long, around a pound.

FOOD VALUE: Considered excellent, but take care.

GAME QUALITIES: Poor.

TACKLE: Any sort of bottom-fishing tackle.

LURES AND BAITS: Cut pieces of fish or squid.

OTHER NAMES:

Sculpin
Lapon

RANGE: *From central California to Baja California, Mexico, including the Gulf of California.*

WHERE TO FISH: *Over rocky bottom and near kelp beds, from near shore to at least 300 feet deep.*

Canary Rockfish

Sebastes pinniger

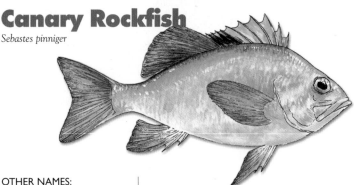

OTHER NAMES:

Fantail Rockfish
Orange Rockfish
Red Snapper

RANGE: *Alaska to Baja California, Mexico.*

WHERE TO FISH: *Most are caught in 100 feet of water or more, although small ones do roam close to shore. They like hard bottom but generally hang above the bottom by several feet.*

DESCRIPTION: Overall color is bright yellow to orange with gray mottling. Three orange stripes run across the head. The fins are also orange.

SIZE: Runs to perhaps 9 pounds, although it typically weighs 3-6 pounds. World record 10 pounds.

FOOD VALUE: Excellent.

GAME QUALITIES: Poor; generally overmatched.

TACKLE: Can be caught at times on fairly light spinning or baitcasting gear, but far more often falls to heavy rigs.

LURES AND BAITS: Cut baits. Metallic and plastic-tail jigs can also produce.

Chilipepper

Sebastes goodei

OTHER NAMES:

Chili Cod

RANGE: *British Columbia to Baja California, Mexico.*

WHERE TO FISH: *Adults seem to prefer deep rocky reefs, but are caught over soft bottom as well—most often in depths of 100 feet or much more, although young fish and a few adults do roam close to shore.*

DESCRIPTION: Overall hue is pinkish to copper, with a vivid red area running along the lateral line. The lower jaw projects farther than the upper. Tail is concave.

SIZE: Most run 2-4 pounds.

FOOD VALUE: Very good.

GAME QUALITIES: Poor.

TACKLE: Bottom-fishing gear.

LURES AND BAITS: Small live or dead fish, or pieces of cut bait. Metallic spoons or jigs are productive lures.

China Rockfish

Sebastes nebulosus

DESCRIPTION: This colorful species has a wide yellow stripe running from the tail along the lateral line, then "climbing" to the dorsal fin.

SIZE: Seldom larger than 1 or 2 pounds. May reach 5 pounds on rare occasion. World record 3 pounds, 11 ounces.

FOOD VALUE: Fillets are very small but of excellent taste.

GAME QUALITIES: Willing but without much muscle.

TACKLE: China Rockfish are not targeted and so are caught on the full variety of light tackle.

LURES AND BAITS: Cut fish or squid, plus lures such as small jigs, small spoons and swimming plugs.

OTHER NAMES:

Yellowstripe Rockfish
Cod
Rock Cod
China Cod

RANGE: *Alaska to southern California.*

WHERE TO FISH: *Caught only occasionally and usually near the coastline over rocky bottom and around points.*

Copper Rockfish

Sebastes caurinus

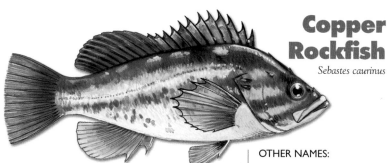

DESCRIPTION: Similar to Brown Rockfish, but it has a white streak along rear half of the lateral line.

SIZE: Averages a couple of pounds. Sometimes reaches 5 or 6 pounds. World record 6 pounds, 1 ounce.

FOOD VALUE: Very good.

GAME QUALITIES: A pretty rough tussler when caught in the shallows on light gear.

TACKLE: Spinning and baitcasting inshore; medium ocean gear offshore.

LURES AND BAITS: Chunks of small fish pay off as well as jigs, spoons and swimming lures.

OTHER NAMES:

Whitebelly Rockfish
Yellowbacked Rockfish
Rock Cod

RANGE: *Basically from Alaska to northern California, but strays as far as Baja California, Mexico.*

WHERE TO FISH: *Often caught close inshore around kelp, rocks or other obstructions, but is found to depths of about 400 feet.*

Cowcod

Sebastes levis

OTHER NAMES:

Cow Rockfish

RANGE: *Central California to central Baja California, Mexico.*

WHERE TO FISH: *Offshore rocks and banks in depths of 300 to 1,000 feet. Most are probably taken in 500-600 feet.*

DESCRIPTION: The huge head and bright color make identification a snap—as does sheer size. Overall color is deep yellow to orange and the eyes are gold.

SIZE: The giant among Rockfishes, the Cow Cod often runs 10 to 20 pounds and can reach 30 pounds or more.

FOOD VALUE: Excellent.

GAME QUALITIES: Good strength but, despite large size, it is usually overpowered by heavy gear.

TACKLE: Heavy bottom-fishing outfits.

LURES AND BAITS: Large cut baits (fish or squid) or whole dead fish, such as Herring.

Grass Rockfish

Sebastes rastrelliger

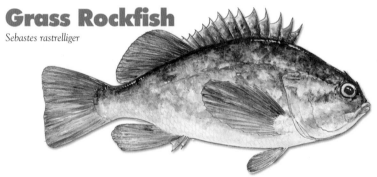

RANGE: *Oregon to Baja California, Mexico.*

WHERE TO FISH: *This is mostly a shallow-water fish and an angling favorite of shorefishermen in particular. However, it is also frequently caught in water as deep as 150 feet. As the name indicates, it can be found in grass beds and around kelp, but it also hangs out, like other Rockfishes, over hard bottom and around obstacles.*

DESCRIPTION: Chunky body is very dark; olive above, mottled with lighter green, or gray, on the sides and white belly. The caudal peduncle is very thick.

SIZE: Averages around 2 pounds but is fairly common at 5 pounds and can push 10 pounds.

FOOD VALUE: Very good.

GAME QUALITIES: Outstanding for its size.

TACKLE: For surf or jetty fishing, surf tackle does a fine job, but lighter gear can be put to good use.

LURES AND BAITS: Will hit a variety of small lures, such as jigs and spoons, along with natural baits.

Greenspotted Rockfish

Sebastes chlorostictus

DESCRIPTION: In addition to the sprinkling of green spots that give this fish its name, it is also identifiable by four or five white or pink spots on its back and sides. Overall color is tan or yellow. The fins are pink.

SIZE: Averages under 5 pounds but occasionally reaches 8 or 10 pounds. World record 2 pounds, 3 ounces.

FOOD VALUE: Very good.

GAME QUALITIES: Poor on heavy tackle.

TACKLE: Bottom-fishing gear.

LURES AND BAITS: Chunks of cut fish or squid. Will take heavy jigs bounced on bottom.

RANGE: From Washington to central Baja California, Mexico. Most plentiful from central California northward.

WHERE TO FISH: Deep water from 150 to 300 feet or more. Usually taken over soft bottom.

Kelp Rockfish

Sebastes atrovirens

DESCRIPTION: Mottled coloration is usually in shades of pale tan to brown, but is changeable in different environments.

SIZE: Averages 10-12 inches; maximum perhaps 18 inches.

FOOD VALUE: Very good.

GAME QUALITIES: Poor.

TACKLE: Any bottom-fishing tackle.

LURES AND BAITS: Small live fish or crabs, or cut pieces of fish and squid.

OTHER NAMES:

Roundhead Rockfish Garrupa

RANGE: Central California to central Baja California, Mexico.

WHERE TO FISH: Kelp beds in fairly shallow water. Seldom found deeper than about 150 feet and most common at 50 feet or less.

Olive Rockfish

Sebastes serranoides

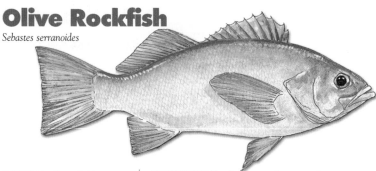

RANGE: *Northern California to central Baja California, Mexico.*

WHERE TO FISH: *They orient to kelp beds or reefs, but may be found anywhere from the surface to the bottom. Most are taken in shallow or fairly shallow water, less than 50 feet.*

DESCRIPTION: Color is olive, shading to tan on lower sides. Fins are olive with shadings of yellow.

SIZE: Most run 1 or 2 pounds; may reach 6 or 8 pounds. World record 3 pounds, 9 ounces.

FOOD VALUE: Very good.

GAME QUALITIES: Pretty tough on light tackle.

TACKLE: Spinning and baitcasting gear provide both best action and best sport.

LURES AND BAITS: Small baitfish, cut fish or squid, plus jigs and spoons as light as possible, given the particular fishing depth.

Quillback Rockfish

Sebastes maliger

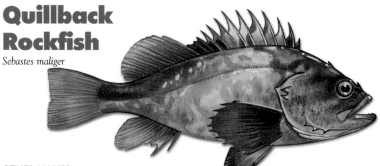

OTHER NAMES:

Orangespotted Rockfish
Speckled Rockfish

RANGE: *Alaska to central California.*

WHERE TO FISH: *Many are found in water 50 feet deep or less but habitat extends to around 700 feet. Quillbacks prefer rocky bottoms and reefs, alone or in small schools.*

DESCRIPTION: Mottled brown color with blotches of yellow on top and dorsal fin. Orange spots on lower sides.

SIZE: Most run 2-3 pounds; can reach 6 or 7 pounds. World record 7 pounds, 4 ounces.

FOOD VALUE: Excellent.

GAME QUALITIES: Strikes hard but not a tough fighter.

TACKLE: Heavy spinning and baitcasting outfits and light ocean outfits are often useful.

LURES AND BAITS: Quillbacks hit a wide variety of lures, topped by heavy spoons and jigs.

Redbanded Rockfish

Sebastes babcocki

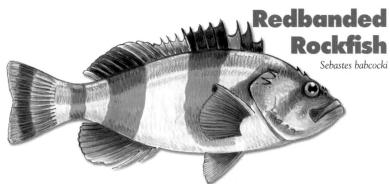

DESCRIPTION: Nearly identical to the Flag Rockfish (*S. rubrivinctus*). The Redbanded is larger and light pink to red with four vertical bars of darker red on the body. In Flag Rockfish, all bars are widely separated.

SIZE: 2 or 3 pounds on average; may reach 10 pounds. World record 9 pounds, 12 ounces.

FOOD VALUE: Both are very good.

GAME QUALITIES: Poor.

TACKLE: Bottom-fishing gear.

LURES AND BAITS: Cut baits do most of the work.

RANGE: Alaska to southern California, but most common from San Francisco northward.

WHERE TO FISH: Unlike most Rockfishes, the Redbanded is often taken on soft bottom, but mixes with other species over hard bottom types as well. Found from about 150 feet to well over 1,000 feet. The Flag is often caught in somewhat shallower water.

Redstripe Rockfish

Sebastes proriger

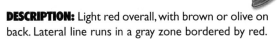

DESCRIPTION: Light red overall, with brown or olive on back. Lateral line runs in a gray zone bordered by red.

SIZE: Averages 2-4 pounds; tops around 10.

FOOD VALUE: Very good.

GAME QUALITIES: When caught on reasonably light line, as it frequently is, it can give a good account of itself.

TACKLE: Spinning and baitcasting gear are best in up to perhaps 100 feet of water.

LURES AND BAITS: Cut fish and squid for bottom fishing. Fast-sinking lures in shallow water.

RANGE: Alaska to southern California.

WHERE TO FISH: Generally sticks close to hard or rocky bottom in depths of 40 feet to as much as 900 feet. Tends to run shallower in more northerly portions of its range.

Rosy Rockfish

Sebastes rosaceus

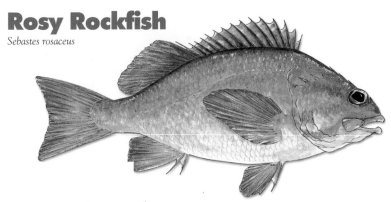

RANGE: *Washington to Baja California, Mexico, but caught mostly off California.*

WHERE TO FISH: *Fairly shallow water, say 15-50 feet, over rocky bottom and around kelp.*

DESCRIPTION: The sides are red, tinged with yellow. Four to five light blotches bordered in purple dot the back. A purplish band runs across the head. Fins are orange.

SIZE: Averages around 1 foot in length.

FOOD VALUE: Small fillets but excellent eating.

GAME QUALITIES: Poor.

TACKLE: Any sort of light tackle with small weights and hooks.

LURES AND BAITS: Cut fish, shrimp and squid.

Silvergray Rockfish

Sebastes brevispinis

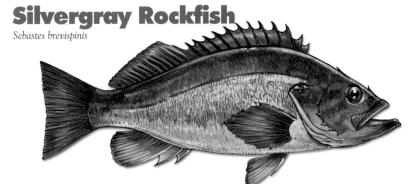

RANGE: *Alaska to Baja California, Mexico.*

WHERE TO FISH: *Uncommon and not targetable, most are caught in mixed bags with other Rockfishes over hard, crevice-strewn bottom, from near shore to about 400 feet.*

DESCRIPTION: Greenish to silver gray, tinged with orange or pink on the underside. Dark lips. Long lower jaw protrudes beyond upper jaw. Tail is slightly concave.

SIZE: Usually up to 5 pounds or so. Can exceed 10 pounds. World record 10 pounds, 6 ounces.

FOOD VALUE: Even better than most Rockfishes.

GAME QUALITIES: Poor on heavy tackle.

TACKLE: Any bottom-fishing gear.

LURES AND BAITS: Chunks of cut herring or other fish are deadly. Jigs and spoons also produce.

Speckled Rockfish

Sebastes ovalis

DESCRIPTION: Coloration is tan with a pink tinge. Small black spots.

SIZE: Averages 1-2 pounds. Fish over 4 pounds are exceptional. World record 2 pounds, 11 ounces.

FOOD VALUE: Excellent.

GAME QUALITIES: Poor; too small to resist much.

TACKLE: Usually caught on bottom-fishing gear, but heavy spinning and baitcasting can be used.

LURES AND BAITS: Small live or dead fish, or pieces of cut bait. Metallic spoons or jigs are productive lures.

OTHER NAMES:

Spotted Bass

RANGE: Northern California to northern Baja California, Mexico; most common in southern California.

WHERE TO FISH: Common over rocky areas, mostly in 60-500 feet of water.

Tiger Rockfish

Sebastes nigrocinctus

DESCRIPTION: Light pink to red in color with five or six dark red vertical bars on the body and another dark bar extending from each eye.

SIZE: Averages 2 or 3 pounds; sometimes exceeds 5 pounds. World record 4 pounds, 14 ounces.

FOOD VALUE: Very good.

GAME QUALITIES: Poor, although much better if taken in shallow water.

TACKLE: Bottom-fishing gear.

LURES AND BAITS: Various cut baits, mostly of small fish, plus deep-sinking jigs.

OTHER NAMES:

Banded Rockfish
Tiger Cod

RANGE: Alaska to central California, but most common off Canada and Alaska.

WHERE TO FISH: Sometimes caught fairly close to shore but far more numerous over deep reefs in depths of about 150-800 feet.

Vermilion Rockfish

Sebastes miniatus

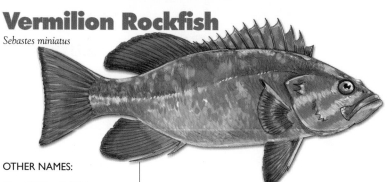

OTHER NAMES:

Red Rockfish
Red Snapper

RANGE: *British Columbia to central Baja California, Mexico.*

WHERE TO FISH: *Vermilions are found from near shore out to 500 feet or more, but shallow water over rocks or other hard bottom is the preferred habitat.*

DESCRIPTION: Dark red in color, with sides mottled in gray. The mouth and fins have black edges.

SIZE: Usually 2-5 pounds, but not uncommon at 10 pounds. World record 12 pounds.

FOOD VALUE: Very good.

GAME QUALITIES: Those taken on light tackle are rugged fighters that usually dig hard for the bottom.

TACKLE: Spinning and baitcasting are the most sporting.

LURES AND BAITS: Always hungry, they will hit natural baits without much selectivity.

Widow Rockfish

Sebastes entomelas

RANGE: *Gulf of Alaska to Baja California, Mexico.*

WHERE TO FISH: *Adults are always caught offshore in water from 100 feet deep to more than 1,000, but may hold well above bottom over rocks or humps. Juveniles school inshore but are seldom noticed and often not even identified, due to their different color, light with reddish streaks.*

DESCRIPTION: Color is yellowish brown above, shading to white below, often tinged with red. The dorsal fin is tan and the others are dark brown to black.

SIZE: Occasionally tops 10 pounds, average 3-6 pounds.

FOOD VALUE: Very good.

GAME QUALITIES: Poor.

TACKLE: Bottom-fishing gear, large sinkers.

LURES AND BAITS: Cut pieces of fish or crustacean are best natural offerings. They will hit heavy jigs, and occasionally a trolled Salmon lure.

Yelloweye Rockfish

Sebastes ruberrimus

DESCRIPTION: Overall rosy red with large yellow eyes. Smaller fish have a light stripe along the lateral line.

SIZE: A large Rockfish, many caught in the 5- to 10-pound range. World record 39 pounds, 4 ounces.

FOOD VALUE: Very good.

GAME QUALITIES: Typically rather poor—like other Rockfishes caught deep on heavy equipment.

TACKLE: Stout bottom-fishing outfits.

LURES AND BAITS: Small whole fish, cut baits and heavy metallic jigs.

OTHER NAMES:

Rapshead Rockfish
Turkey Red Rockfish
Red Rockfish
Red Snapper

RANGE: *Alaska to southern California.*

WHERE TO FISH: *Nearly all are caught in water deeper than 150 feet. They range seaward to depths of well over 1,000 feet.*

Yellowtail Rockfish

Sebastes flavidus

DESCRIPTION: Color is olive to greenish brown with light mottling on the back. Sides are light and the fins are yellowish green. Ventral fins have orange tips.

SIZE: Tops out at about 10 pounds; most run 2-5 pounds. World record 5 pounds, 8 ounces.

FOOD VALUE: Very good.

GAME QUALITIES: Pretty tough fighter on light gear.

TACKLE: Inshore—spinning and baitcasting outfits or surf tackle. Offshore—medium to heavy bottom-fishing gear.

LURES AND BAITS: Small live baitfish or cut chunks of fish lead the pack, but will hit various artificials.

RANGE: *Alaska to southern California.*

WHERE TO FISH: *Widely found from shore out to around 1,000 feet. Inshore anglers often find them schooled in open water, but close to rocks, points or dropoffs. They also school heavily offshore, over reefs.*

ish of the Cod family, along with their close relatives the Hakes, are found in cold northern waters all around the world, but are not well represented in the eastern Pacific. The four covered in this chapter are our only examples, and none is any great pet of sport fishermen, even though all are happily accepted when more prestigious prey is not in season or not cooperating. On the commercial side, it is a different story, particularly with the Pollock, which is rendered into a pure protein product called surimi and then molded and flavored to imitate crab or shrimp. The Tomcod and Hake are junior members of this group, notable mostly because of their availability to shorebound fishermen, especially young anglers. The Tomcod is also a fish-fry favorite. Although larger on average than Tomcod, Hake are looked upon with less gustatory enthusiasm.

Cods and Kin

Pacific Cod

Pacific Hake

Pacific Tomcod

Walleye Pollock

Pacific Cod

Gadus macrocephalus

OTHER NAMES:

Gray Cod
True Cod

RANGE: *Alaska to southern California; far more plentiful from Oregon northward.*

WHERE TO FISH: *Over hard bottom in as little as 30 or 40 feet (during colder months), and on out to depths that challenge sportfishing capabilities.*

DESCRIPTION: Three dorsal fins and a long chin barbel help identify the Cod, which is brown to gray in color with blotches on the upper sides.

SIZE: Commonly caught in a wide range of sizes from a couple of pounds to 15 pounds or so, and rarely to 30 pounds or more. World record 35 pounds.

FOOD VALUE: Good but tends to softness.

GAME QUALITIES: Not bad when caught on reasonably light tackle, but most are overpowered on heavy gear.

TACKLE: Any sort of bottom-fishing gear.

LURES AND BAITS: Various natural baits work well, including whole and cut small fish, crabs, octopus and squid. Many Cod are taken on lures, particularly on metallic jigs yo-yoed on and near bottom.

Pacific Hake

Merluccius productus

DESCRIPTION: Although in a different family, the Hake is superficially similar to the Cod but easily distinguishable by the large mouth with teeth, and by the second dorsal fin, which is long and notched rather than divided into separate fins. Color is silvery with small black spots on back.

SIZE: Most run a couple of pounds. Maximum might be 10 or so. World record 2 pounds, 2 ounces.

FOOD VALUE: Fair; meat is soft.

GAME QUALITIES: Poor.

TACKLE: Not usually targeted. Lightest gear is best.

LURES AND BAITS: Hits artificials including small jigs and spoons, as well as small fish and cut baits.

RANGE: British Columbia, Canada, to the Gulf of California, Mexico.

WHERE TO FISH: Often an incidental catch while Salmon trolling or bottom fishing, but also caught near shore and from piers, especially at night.

Pacific Tomcod

Microgadus proximus

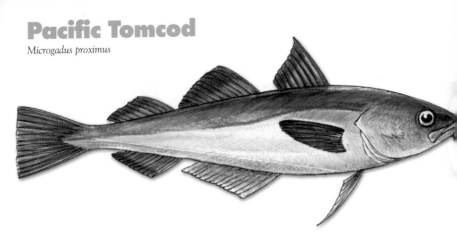

RANGE: *Alaska to central California; more common in northern part of range.*

WHERE TO FISH: *Most sport catches are made from boats near shore, or from docks, piers and banks.*

DESCRIPTION: Similar in outline to the Cod, but has no patterns on the sides and is much smaller. The chin barbel is also proportionately smaller.

SIZE: Most are under 1 pound and few run as much as 2 pounds.

FOOD VALUE: An excellent panfish.

GAME QUALITIES: Poor because of small size.

TACKLE: Poles and very light spinning gear.

LURES AND BAITS: Cut baits of fish or shellfish presented on small hooks.

Walleye Pollock

Theragra chalcogramma

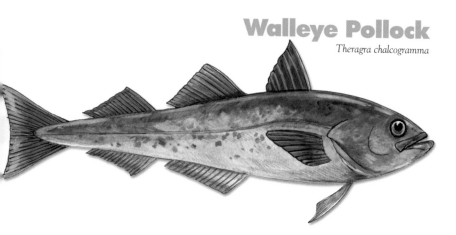

DESCRIPTION: Generally more slender than the Cod, although similar in overall appearance. The chin barbel is very short, and absent in many specimens. The lower jaw extends slightly beyond the upper jaw, unlike the Cod. Color is greenish or brown on top, silvery on the sides. Markings, if present, are faint.

SIZE: Common around 2 or 3 pounds. A few may exceed 5 pounds.

FOOD VALUE: Fair; little flavor and the flesh is soft.

GAME QUALITIES: Not much of a fighter.

TACKLE: Any sort of bottom-fishing gear.

LURES AND BAITS: Various natural baits work well, including whole and cut small fish, crabs, octopus and squid. Also strikes metallic jigs near bottom.

OTHER NAMES:

Pacific Pollock
Bigeye Pollock

RANGE: Alaska to central California; much more common in northern sector of its range.

WHERE TO FISH: Mixes with the Cod and the two are often caught interchangeably.

The Lingcod, like the Rock Cod (Rockfish), is not really a Cod at all. In fact, if the two should happen to meet face to face, the Lingcod would probably scare a true Cod into the nearest hole, thanks to its cavernous mouth and formidable dentition. Scary looking though it may be, the Lingcod is still one of the species most eagerly sought by onshore and nearshore anglers from Oregon to Alaska. Whether the Lingcod is a member of the Greenling family is debated by some biologists, who would put it in a family of its own. Anglers, however, see many similarities and only one major difference—the considerably greater size of the Lingcod. All of them are just a step removed from the Rockfishes, which have spines on their heads; the Lingcod and Greenlings do not. Rock Cods and Lingcods frequently share mixed bags, although the latter is always the big prize. One thing that might be a bit disconcerting to fishermen unfamiliar with these fish is that their flesh is green—at least before being cooked. Afterwards it is white and flaky and ranked among the best.

Lingcod and Greenlings

Kelp Greenling

Lingcod

Rock Greenling

Whitespotted Greenling

Kelp Greenling

Hexagrammos decagrammus

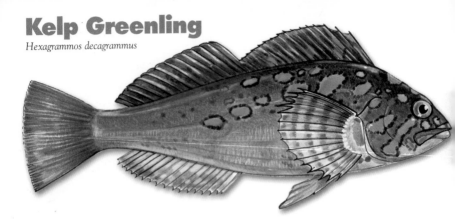

OTHER NAMES:

Kelp Trout
Sea Trout

RANGE: *Alaska to southern California; far more common from central California northward.*

WHERE TO FISH: *Prefers inshore waters around rocks, kelp and points, but may also be found over sand at times.*

DESCRIPTION: Body color is gray to brown. Females wear reddish or brown spots all over, while males have blue spots, each ringed with smaller brown spots, on forward part of body only.

SIZE: Most catches run 2-3 pounds; maximum is perhaps 4 pounds. World record 3 pounds, 2 ounces.

FOOD VALUE: Excellent.

GAME QUALITIES: Gives a fine battle on light line.

TACKLE: Light spinning or baitcasting gear will provide the most sport.

LURES AND BAITS: Natural baits produce the most action—cut fish or squid, shrimp and marine worms are all good. Small jigs and slowly fished spoons are also productive.

Lingcod

Ophiodon elongatus

DESCRIPTION: This is a long and fearsome-looking fish, with large mouth and many sharp teeth. The gill rakers are also sharp, so take care in handling. The color is variable, ranging from gray to green to blue, with prominent blotches and spots.

SIZE: Generally runs 10-20 pounds but is not uncommon at 30 or 40 pounds and has been reported to more than 100. World record 75 pounds, 12 ounces.

FOOD VALUE: Excellent. Flesh is often green but whitens when cooked.

GAME QUALITIES: A strong, bulldogging battler, but best on light line. Unlike Rockfishes, it has no air bladder and can resist from bottom to top when hooked in deep water.

TACKLE: Any sort of bottom-fishing or jigging gear; salmon tackle is often used.

LURES AND BAITS: Feed mostly on other fishes but also take crustaceans, octopus and squid. Live fish are more likely to produce a big specimen, and Lingcod often grab hooked fish that are being hauled up. Large cut baits are the norm on many boats. Metallic jigs are also very productive when yo-yoed near bottom.

OTHER NAMES:

Cutlass Cod

RANGE: *Alaska to northern Baja California, Mexico, but much more common northward of central California.*

WHERE TO FISH: *Over rocky bottom, from close inshore in northern waters to mostly well offshore in California.*

Rock Greenling

Hexagrammos lagocephalus

OTHER NAMES:

Red Greenling
Rock Trout

RANGE: *Alaska to central California.*

WHERE TO FISH: *Rocky areas, pilings and other obstructions close to shore; many are caught by land-bound anglers.*

DESCRIPTION: Color is green to brown with dark mottling, often bright red, on the sides. Inside of the mouth is blue.

SIZE: Most catches run 2-3 pounds; maximum is perhaps 5 or 6 pounds. World record 1 pound, 13 ounces.

FOOD VALUE: Excellent.

GAME QUALITIES: Gives a fine battle on light line.

TACKLE: Light spinning or baitcasting gear will provide the most sport.

LURES AND BAITS: Natural baits produce the most action—cut fish or squid, shrimp, and marine worms are all good. Small jigs and other lures can also get fish.

Whitespotted Greenling

Hexagrammos stellari

DESCRIPTION: Color is generally light brown with darker blotches. Body is liberally sprinkled with white spots.

SIZE: Averages 1 or 2 pounds; seldom tops 3 pounds.

FOOD VALUE: Excellent.

GAME QUALITIES: Small but scrappy on light gear.

TACKLE: Light spinning outfits are best.

LURES AND BAITS: Natural baits produce the most action—cut fish or squid, shrimp and marine worms. Small jigs get strikes as well.

OTHER NAMES:

Common Greenling

RANGE: Alaska to Puget Sound.

WHERE TO FISH: Inshore around pilings, rocks or grass.

Freshwater fishermen know Sculpins as secretive little fellows that hide among the rocks to avoid getting gulped down by Bass and Trout. But that's only one branch of the family. Sculpins of many kinds inhabit most cold and temperate waters all around the world, and in coastal salt waters of the Pacific a few of them grow large enough to be of keen interest to sport fishermen. They are related to the Rockfishes and Lingcod and share much of the same habitat. Like the Scorpionfish they have spiny heads, but they also sport large and fanlike pectoral fins. At the top of the heap for size, and therefore angler appeal, is the Cabezon. The Irish Lords are not prime targets but are caught often enough in mixed bags to gain attention. The Sculpins covered in this chapter represent only a few of the many kinds found along our Pacific Coast, but are the only ones of any interest at all to fishermen. Most of the rest, like their freshwater kin, dart about in rocky tidal shallows.

The Sculpins

Cabezon

Pacific Staghorn Sculpin

Red Irish Lord

Yellow Irish Lord

Cabezon

Scorpaenichthys marmoratus

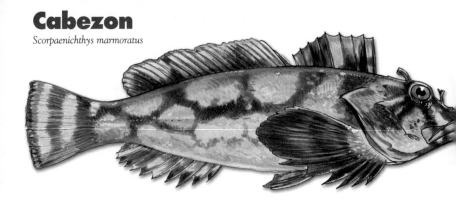

OTHER NAMES:

Blue Cod
Bull Cod
Giant Marble
  Sculpin
Bullhead

RANGE: *Alaska to northern Baja California, Mexico.*

WHERE TO FISH: *Mostly along rocky shores and over rocks or grass beds a short distance offshore, but they are also taken on rocky bottom out to about 300 feet.*

DESCRIPTION: Color is mottled brown, reddish or green above and pale below. The head is wide and spiny and the mouth is large. Pectorals are fanlike. Spines on head.

SIZE: Common at 2-8 pounds; not rare to 10 or 15 pounds and can reach perhaps 30 pounds. World record 23 pounds.

FOOD VALUE: Very good; flesh is quite firm and thought by many to taste like lobster or crab. But discard the roe as it can cause severe illness.

GAME QUALITIES: An outstanding battler on light or medium casting tackle.

TACKLE: Spinning and baitcasting gear offer best sport inshore; bottom-fishing gear offshore.

LURES AND BAITS: Natural diet is heavy on crab, but they will take shrimp, squid and whole or cut Herring and other baitfishes. They are also ready strikers on small jigs and spoons.

Pacific Staghorn Sculpin

Leptocottus armatus

DESCRIPTION: Scaleless. Color is tan to brown above, yellowish below. Fins are yellow with dark bars. Dark spot at rear of first dorsal fin.

SIZE: Less than 1 pound on average; seldom reaches 2 pounds.

FOOD VALUE: Too scrawny to bother with.

GAME QUALITIES: Poor.

TACKLE: Light spinning.

LURES AND BAITS: Nearly any sort of small cut bait, whether fish, squid, worm or shrimp. Small artificials are often taken as well.

OTHER NAMES:

**Smooth Sculpin
Bullhead**

RANGE: Alaska to central Baja California, Mexico.

WHERE TO FISH: Not often targeted, except as bait for Striped Bass, but easily caught inshore and in bays and coastal rivers. Often a nuisance to anglers seeking larger prey.

Red Irish Lord

Hemilepidotus hemilepidotus

RANGE: *Alaska to central California; most common in Alaska and British Columbia.*

WHERE TO FISH: *Around inshore rocks and out to perhaps 15 feet.*

DESCRIPTION: Color is reddish brown with brown, black and white blotches on upper sides. Several dark saddles across top. Head is rough and horny, typical of Sculpins.

SIZE: Usually a pound or less; may occasionally hit 3 pounds. World record 2 pounds, 7 ounces.

FOOD VALUE: Excellent, if not very meaty.

GAME QUALITIES: Scrappy but a lightweight.

TACKLE: Spinning and baitcasting gear offer best sport.

LURES AND BAITS: Shrimp, squid and cut fish. They are also ready strikers on small jigs and spoons.

Yellow Irish Lord

Hemilepidotus jordani

DESCRIPTION: Color is yellowish to brown with four dark bars on top and mottling on sides.

SIZE: Most run a pound or less; 2-pounders are unusual.

FOOD VALUE: Excellent but skimpy.

GAME QUALITIES: Not much.

TACKLE: Spinning and baitcasting gear offer best sport.

LURES AND BAITS: Shrimp, squid and cut fish. They also take small jigs.

RANGE: Alaska.

WHERE TO FISH: Not often targeted; caught in mixed bags from shoreline rocks and out to about 300 feet.

Striped Bass are a bit out of place in this grouping, sharing only the name of "Bass." But then, they are a bit out of place in the Pacific Ocean, too. Or they once were. Now, more than 100 years after being introduced from the Atlantic, they have become well acclimated and as popular among anglers over here as are their ancestors across the continent. Scientists classify Stripers in a family labeled "Temperate Basses." The other species in this chapter all belong to a different family, one called, simply, "Sea Basses." Most of these are tropical in habitat and wear "Grouper" as part of their common name, but there are many prominent exceptions, particularly in California, where the various Kelp and Sand Basses rank among the leading sport species, and the Giant Sea Bass is still present, if rare. One more fish—a "Bass" in name only—must be mentioned here, even though it is covered elsewhere (Chapter 5). That is the impressively large White Sea Bass, which actually is a member of the Croaker family.

Basses and Groupers

Barred Sand Bass

Black Sea Bass

Broomtail Grouper

Flag Cabrilla

Giant Hawkfish

Goldspotted Sand Bass

Goliath Grouper

Gulf Coney

Gulf Grouper

Kelp Bass

Leopard Grouper

Panama Graysby

Sawtail Grouper

Snowy Grouper

Spotted Cabrilla

Spotted Sand Bass

Starstudded Grouper

Striped Bass

Barred Sand Bass

Paralabrax nebulifer

RANGE: *Central California to southern Baja California, Mexico; most popular off southern California.*

WHERE TO FISH: *Likes sandy area or patches near rocks, from the shoreline out to about 100 feet, sometimes deeper.*

DESCRIPTION: Top is greenish; lower part dingy white. There are bars on the sides, but no spots. There are yellow spots, however, on the head. The tail is square.

SIZE: Averages a pound or two; reaches 7 or 8 pounds. World record 13 pounds, 3 ounces.

FOOD VALUE: Very good.

GAME QUALITIES: A good scrapper on light line.

TACKLE: Baitcasting or spinning; long rods useful.

LURES AND BAITS: Anchovy and squid top a long list of naturals deployed by party boats and private craft. Although not as good a lure fish as the Kelp Bass, it often is taken trolling jigs or crankbaits in open areas, or casting around breakwaters.

Black Sea Bass

Stereolepis gigas

DESCRIPTION: This giant is gray or dark brown on top and sides, whitish or yellowish below. Dark patches on the sides disappear shortly after landing. The tail is slightly concave. The rays of the ventral fins are black with white separating membranes.

SIZE: Very long lived, this fish has been recorded to more than 500 pounds and rumored to reach 1,000. In the past, 100- to 300-pounders were fairly numerous and 50-pounders were common, but both numbers and sizes have shrunk alarmingly. Now endangered, a zero bag limit is in effect in California at this writing.

FOOD VALUE: No longer available for the table.

GAME QUALITIES: Shows strength but not a great deal of stamina. Catches of fish over 100 pounds on rather light tackle were once made with fair regularity.

TACKLE: Speaking in terms of the past, ocean gear with line testing at least 50 pounds was generally chosen, but many kinds of tackle were used successfully for the average-size fish.

LURES AND BAITS: Very large live baits were the norm. A live Whitefish was one popular choice, but many varieties were used.

OTHER NAMES:

Giant Sea Bass
Southern
  Sea Bass
Pescara

RANGE: *Northern California to Gulf of California, Mexico. Historically, the prime grounds were off the southern California coast.*

WHERE TO FISH: *Occurs on rock bottoms, around kelp beds and along dropoffs. Although some are encountered near shore, the big fish mostly stick to depths of 100 feet or more.*

Broomtail Grouper

Mycteroperca xenarcha

RANGE: *Southern California to Panama.*

WHERE TO FISH: *Although it's a reef-lover like other Groupers, the Broomtail is frequently found inshore, especially in deep channels and holes of mangrove country.*

DESCRIPTION: Color is light brown with elongated streaks of dark brown. The tail is raggedly serrated.

SIZE: Averages perhaps 10-20 pounds, but 40- to 50-pounders are pretty common and the maximum potential is around 200 pounds. World record 100 pounds.

FOOD VALUE: Very good.

GAME QUALITIES: Outstanding battler, especially when hooked inshore or in fairly shallow water.

TACKLE: Light ocean trolling or standup tackle with lines to 50-pound test; also baitcasting and spinning outfits.

LURES AND BAITS: In reasonably shallow water the Broomtail will hit many different casting lures, including surface plugs. Most, however, are caught either trolling with diving plugs or weighted trolling lures, or by still-fishing with live baits or large cut baits.

Flag Cabrilla

Epinephelus labriformis

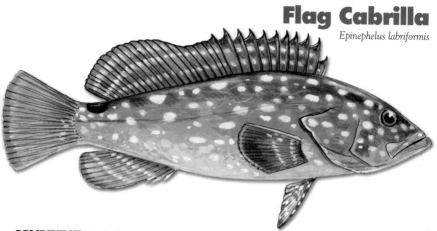

DESCRIPTION: Body is brown or reddish and spectacularly marked with vivid white spots, large on the sides and head, smaller on the fins. The tail is square or slightly rounded. Distinctive black blotch at the top of the caudal peduncle.

SIZE: Averages 1-2 pounds; may reach 5 pounds.

FOOD VALUE: Excellent, though small.

GAME QUALITIES: Hard striker without the heft to back up its aggressiveness.

TACKLE: Light or ultralight spinning makes a good match.

LURES AND BAITS: Various jigs and other small lures, including shallow crankbaits. Many natural baits work, but crab and cut fish are the best.

OTHER NAMES:

Flag Grouper
Cabrilla Piedrera
Starry Grouper

RANGE: *Southern Baja California, Mexico, and the Gulf of California to Panama.*

WHERE TO FISH: *Rocky areas, mostly near shore.*

Giant Hawkfish

Cirrhitus rivulatus

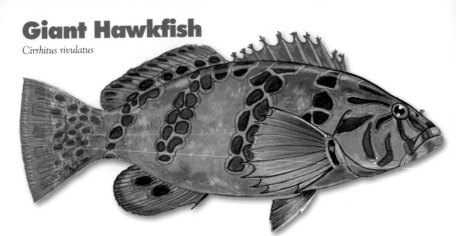

OTHER NAMES:

Harlequin Grouper

RANGE: *Gulf of California, Mexico, to Panama.*

WHERE TO FISH: *Very common around rocks close to shore and in the surf zone but also caught over reefs up to 50 or 60 feet deep.*

DESCRIPTION: This is not a Grouper, although many anglers mistakenly think so because it comes from typical Grouper habitat and is similar in general configuration. The garish coloration features many irregular brown bands, bordered with blue. It also has some reddish spots ringed in white plus two all white spots on the upper body near the back. The head and jaws are large.

SIZE: Usually from one-half pound to 2 pounds; may reach 5 or 6 pounds. World record 9 pounds, 3 ounces.

FOOD VALUE: Good.

GAME QUALITIES: Mostly a curiosity to anglers, it is often caught while fishing deep for bigger prey, or while casting around the shoreline rocks.

TACKLE: Not targeted; often caught with casting tackle near rocky shores.

LURES AND BAITS: Avidly hits most small casting lures, or small natural baitfish.

Goldspotted Sand Bass

Paralabrax auroguttatus

DESCRIPTION: Similar in its greenish color to the Spotted Sand Bass, but it is generally smaller and has bright yellow elongated spots. The pectoral fins are yellow and transparent. Third dorsal spine is high.

SIZE: Averages a couple of pounds; tops about 6 pounds. World record 6 pounds.

FOOD VALUE: Very good.

GAME QUALITIES: Poor; usually overmatched in tackle.

TACKLE: Bottom-fishing gear gets most of them, but baitcasting and spinning can sometimes be utilized for deep-jigging.

LURES AND BAITS: Anchovies and other silvery bait-fishes, squid, artificial jigs.

RANGE: Mostly in the Gulf of California, Mexico. Also the outer coast of Baja California and, rarely, southern California.

WHERE TO FISH: Rocky bottom or sand patches near rocks in 100-200 feet of water.

Goliath Grouper

Epinephelus itajara

OTHER NAMES:

Jewfish
Giant Sea Bass
Mero

RANGE: *Gulf of California, Mexico, to Panama. Although endangered in parts of the Atlantic, it is not nearly so heavily pressured along the Pacific Coast of Latin America.*

WHERE TO FISH: *The biggest fish are usually on offshore reefs and dropoffs. Juveniles—and some of the giants too—roam close to shore in deep channels near mangrove roots, rocks or other structure.*

DESCRIPTION: Sometimes confused with the Giant Sea Bass of California (even to one of its common names) this fish is not a close relative but is the largest member of the Grouper clan. Juveniles are brilliantly marked with irregular dark brown blotches against a light brown or gray background, extending from head to tail. Numerous black spots are usually present as well on head, sides and fins. Adults are easily identified by size alone, but they have the same patterns in more subdued shades of brown that are not so brilliantly contrasted. The tail is round, as are the posterior dorsal, anal and pectoral fins.

SIZE: Common at 200-300 pounds, it often reaches or exceeds 500. Maximum potential is possibly 1,000 pounds. World record 680 pounds.

FOOD VALUE: Very good at all sizes.

GAME QUALITIES: Very difficult to land on any size line in most settings. If hooked in reasonably open water, as they sometimes are, their strength makes for a long battle, but big ones have been taken by experienced anglers on very light lines, even down to 12- or 20-pound test.

TACKLE: Heavy ocean trolling or standup gear.

LURES AND BAITS: Outsize live baits, such as Jack and Snapper, weighing up to 5 pounds. Dead whole fish are accepted as well. Actually, baits weighing as much as 15 or 20 pounds are not too large for big Jewfish, but can be difficult for the angler to handle. That's why somewhat smaller baits are generally chosen.

Gulf Coney

Epinephelus acanthistius

DESCRIPTION: Strikingly colored a deep red overall, with black caudal, anal and second dorsal fins. Several rays of the first dorsal are long and plume-like when erect.

SIZE: Averages around 8 or 10 pounds; sometimes tops 30 pounds.

FOOD VALUE: Excellent.

GAME QUALITIES: A strong and determined battler that must be heavily pressured if the angler is to win.

TACKLE: Not generally targeted but suitable for any sort of good Grouper tackle, meaning bottom-fishing gear with stout rod and rather heavy line.

LURES AND BAITS: Small live fish are excellent but cut fish and squid are also productive. Like other Groupers, will usually hit heavy jigs that come to their attention.

OTHER NAMES:

Red Grouper
Baqueta

RANGE: Gulf of California to Panama.

WHERE TO FISH: Rocky reefs and sand patches at depths of 100-300 feet. Not well known to sportsmen because it seldom ventures to shallow water.

Gulf Grouper

Mycteroperca jordani

RANGE: *Primarily the Gulf of California, Mexico, but also found on the outer coast of Baja California and north to (rarely) southern California.*

WHERE TO FISH: *Numbers are declining, especially of big specimens, but it remains fishable in Mexico. Likes rocks and reefs but sticks to fairly shallow water, usually less than 100 feet and often much less.*

DESCRIPTION: Overall light brown or gray in color with darker blotches and dark streak radiating from the eyes.

SIZE: Most catches fall in the 10- to 25-pound range, but many 50-pounders are taken and an occasional catch will top 100 pounds. The maximum size probably is close to 200 pounds. World record 113 pounds.

FOOD VALUE: Excellent.

GAME QUALITIES: Terrific fighter if hooked a reasonable distance from holes and big rocks.

TACKLE: For bigger and deeper fish, ocean or standup gear with 50-pound line is a good choice. Casting tackle, either baitcasting or spinning, can be used with reasonable chance of success in certain situations.

LURES AND BAITS: Many are caught trolling with diving plugs and other subsurface lures. For still fishing, live small baitfish are best but dead baits will produce. They also respond to deep-fished metallic and leadhead jigs.

Kelp Bass

Paralabrax clathratus

DESCRIPTION: Color is greenish above, white below. Sides marked with numerous white or gray blotches—the "calico" pattern. Breeding males have orange lower jaws.

SIZE: Most weigh 2-4 pounds, although fish to 10 pounds are fairly frequent catches and the maximum is about 15 pounds. World record 14 pounds, 7 ounces.

FOOD VALUE: Very good.

GAME QUALITIES: A fine light-tackle battler.

TACKLE: Spinning and baitcasting gear are fine in most instances, as is surf tackle when fishing from shore or jetty. Long rods and fast reels are the ticket for live-baiting offshore.

LURES AND BAITS: The market list of the Kelp Bass is a long one, covering most of the popular natural baits and a great many artificials. Squid and Anchovy rank near the top, but other baitfishes are seldom refused. Various jigs and artificial squids take many Bass, as do some freshwater bass lures, including artificial worms.

OTHER NAMES:

Calico Bass
Bull Bass

RANGE: *Washington to southern Baja California, Mexico. Far more prominent off southern California than in the rest of its range.*

WHERE TO FISH: *The name says it: Kelp beds hold most of these fish. But they are caught in other environs as well, from shore out to 100 feet or so. They roam from bottom to the surface, but the bigger fish generally stick deep.*

Leopard Grouper

Myceteroperca rosacea

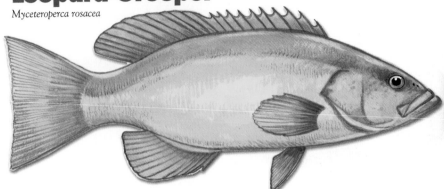

OTHER NAMES:

Golden Grouper

RANGE: *Southwestern Baja California, Mexico plus the Gulf of California and south to Jalisco, Mexico.*

WHERE TO FISH: *Rocky or reef bottom from near shore to about 100 feet.*

DESCRIPTION: Upper body is olive to brown and belly is white or yellowish. Liberally marked with brown spots. Some individuals are a solid golden color.

SIZE: Averages 2-6 pounds. Tops out at about 25 pounds. World record 21 pounds, 4 ounces.

FOOD VALUE: Very good.

GAME QUALITIES: Fine battler against light gear.

TACKLE: Ocean or standup tackle plus stout spinning and baitcasting outfits.

LURES AND BAITS: For still fishing, live Herring or Anchovies are tops. Jigs, spoons and even topwater plugs also get strikes, especially when the fish are feeding in bait schools, as they often do.

Panama Graysby

Epinephelus panamensis

DESCRIPTION: Bands of black and bluish-gray give this fish its tiger-stripe appearance. The head is sprinkled with blue and orange spots and, in adults, there is a large dark spot behind the eye. The tail is rounded.

SIZE: Most run 10-12 inches.

FOOD VALUE: Good but skimpy.

GAME QUALITIES: Because of its aggressive nature it is one of the most-caught fish, frequently striking lures almost as large as itself, but it lacks the size to put up a fight.

TACKLE: Spinning and baitcasting gear.

LURES AND BAITS: Small fish, cut fish, squid. For lures, bottom-bouncing jigs do the job.

OTHER NAMES:

Pacific Graysby
Tiger Grouper
Enjambre

RANGE: *Gulf of California to Panama.*

WHERE TO FISH: *Many are caught from land along rocky shorelines. They are also numerous on coral or rock bottom in depths to 200 feet.*

Sawtail Grouper

Mycteroperca prionura

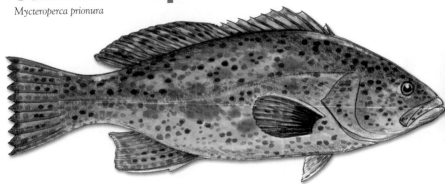

RANGE: *Mexico: Gulf of California to Jalisco, Mexico.*

WHERE TO FISH: *Coral reefs and rocks in fairly shallow water, from about 15 to 100 feet.*

DESCRIPTION: Color is light gray, almost white, with many small black dots and large dark blotches. The tail is evenly serrated, unlike that of the similar Broomtail Grouper, which is ragged.

SIZE: Common at 10-15 pounds; reaches at least 30 pounds. World record 31 pounds.

FOOD VALUE: Excellent.

GAME QUALITIES: Great battler, especially when hooked on light gear.

TACKLE: Light ocean trolling or standup tackle with lines to 50-pound test; also baitcasting and spinning outfits.

LURES AND BAITS: Many are caught trolling with diving plugs and other subsurface lures. For still fishing, live small baitfish are best but dead baits will produce. They also respond to deep-fished metallic and lead-head jigs.

Snowy Grouper

Epinephelus niveatus

DESCRIPTION: Body is rusty brown, liberally sprinkled with white round spots.

SIZE: The average is 5-10 pounds; may reach about 30 pounds. World record 27 pounds, 6 ounces.

FOOD VALUE: Excellent.

GAME QUALITIES: Not often caught on sporting tackle.

TACKLE: Not targeted, sometimes caught by sportsmen at extreme depth with heavy tackle.

LURES AND BAITS: Cut fish or squid.

RANGE: Southern California to Panama.

WHERE TO FISH: Small ones may come into fairly shallow water, 100-200 feet or so, but most of them stay very deep, up to 1,000 feet.

Spotted Cabrilla

Epinephelus analogus

OTHER NAMES:

Spotted Grouper
Cabrilla
Pintada

RANGE: *Southern California to Panama; very plentiful in the Gulf of California, Mexico.*

WHERE TO FISH: *Shallow reefs and patch reefs in up to about 50 feet of water.*

DESCRIPTION: Light brown in color with numerous brown or reddish dots sprinkled over the sides and fins. Looks somewhat like a juvenile Goliath Grouper but is more liberally spotted and the vertical bars are not so prominent.

SIZE: Common at 1-5 pounds; occasionally reaches 25 pounds or more. World record 49 pounds, 3 ounces.

FOOD VALUE: Excellent.

GAME QUALITIES: Good fighter for its size, but often overmatched with heavy tackle.

TACKLE: For sport, the best choice is a reasonably stout spinning or baitcasting outfit.

LURES AND BAITS: This guy seems always ready to please and will greedily take either hair-tail, plastic-tail or metallic jigs yo-yoed near bottom. Crab is main natural diet but it will also take live small fish and cut baits.

Spotted Sand Bass

Paralabrax maculatofasciatus

DESCRIPTION: Easily identified by its numerous small orange or reddish spots, some of them forming vertical bars. Background color is tan or gray.

SIZE: About a pound on average; tops is no more than 3 pounds. World record 2 pounds.

FOOD VALUE: Very good.

GAME QUALITIES: Sporty on light tackle.

TACKLE: Baitcasting or spinning; long rods useful.

LURES AND BAITS: Likes Anchovies and squids. Also caught casting or trolling small lures.

RANGE: Central California to Baja California, Mexico, including the Gulf of California.

WHERE TO FISH: Likes sand or soft bottom but tends to hold near rocks, grass, breakwaters or other structure, from near shore to about 150 feet deep.

Starstudded Grouper

Epinephelus niphobles

OTHER NAMES:

Speckled Grouper

RANGE: *Baja California and the Gulf of California, Mexico, to Panama.*

WHERE TO FISH: *Reef or rock bottom from about 50 feet of water to more than 200 feet.*

DESCRIPTION: Boldly colored in dark brown or black with large white spots. Often confused with the Snowy Grouper but the yellow tail is a distinctive feature.

SIZE: Most run a couple of pounds; a few reach 10 pounds or slightly more.

FOOD VALUE: Good.

GAME QUALITIES: Like most Groupers, tough for its size but usually overmatched in the way of tackle.

TACKLE: Not targeted but occasionally caught on bottom-fishing tackle, or by deep-jigging.

LURES AND BAITS: Any small live or dead fish, plus cut fish and squid. Will take leadhead or metallic jigs.

Striped Bass

Morone saxatilis

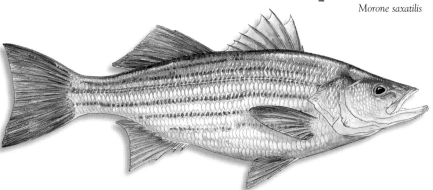

DESCRIPTION: Heavy-bodied with long head and large mouth. Color is dark green to dark gray above, with silvery sides and belly. The sides are marked by bold stripes, regularly spaced and usually unbroken.

SIZE: Reaches 50 pounds or more, but most catches run 5-20 pounds. World record 78 pounds, 8 ounces.

FOOD VALUE: Very good. The flesh is light and rich.

GAME QUALITIES: Stubborn and very strong, the Striper is a tough challenge for the angler, particularly where strong currents are involved.

TACKLE: For deep-trolling and live-baiting, stout salmon or baitcasting rods and reels with good line capacity are advisable. Stout spinning tackle is also a good choice. For shallow fishing, lighter versions of the same gear, plus medium to heavy fly tackle can all be employed.

LURES AND BAITS: Diving plugs and spoons are fine choices for trolling. Casters rely on spoons, topwater plugs and shallow crankbaits for surface and shallow work. Productive flies include large poppers and streamers that resemble shad. As for natural baits, Herring probably get the most play, although other baitfishes may be favored in different areas. Crabs and marine worms also rate high on the Striper's menu.

OTHER NAMES:

Striper
Rockfish
Rock Bass

RANGE: *The anadromous Atlantic Striped Bass was successfully introduced to San Francisco Bay in 1879. It now is caught in fair numbers from the Sacramento Delta to Coos Bay, Oregon, and even wanders farther north on occasion to Washington and Vancouver, B.C. The San Francisco Bay area, however, remains by far the most productive. Unfortunately, sea-run Striper numbers are declining, due to several factors including loss of access to breeding areas. Maintaining a strong fishery in the future will probably require continuing stocking programs, such as have long been in effect for land-locked populations of Stripers.*

WHERE TO FISH: *Bays, rivers and river mouths produce the most Stripers. Although many more are caught from boats— some from very deep water— Stripers are often viable targets for shoreline fishermen, especially around rocks and points.*

Most Snappers can be identified as family members by their prominent canine teeth, and the name "Snapper" comes from the fact that some of them actually seem to snap at the hands (or other body parts) of an unwary fisherman. And if they happen to hit their target, they clamp down hard and hold on doggedly. Some happier characteristics of the Snappers include a generally bright coloration that is heavy on reds and yellows, plus great table appeal and superb game qualities. Snappers take a wide variety of baits and lures but, despite their democratic appetite many of them are among the wariest of biters whenever visibility is good enough to permit a close look at terminal tackle. For their size, Snappers are hard fighters that generally wage a strong, head-shaking tug-of-war against the angler, and those caught in shallow water are also capable of making long and surprisingly fast runs. In the tropics, numerous members of the family roam nearly everywhere from rivers and inshore shallows to far over deep Pacific banks. Only rare stragglers, however, seem to make it as far north as southern California.

The Snappers

Amarillo Snapper

Barred Pargo

Blue-and-Gold Snapper

Colorado Snapper

Jordan's Snapper

Mullet Snapper

Pacific Cubera Snapper

Pacific Red Snapper

Spotted Rose Snapper

Amarillo Snapper

Lutjanus argentiventris

OTHER NAMES:

Yellow Snapper
Pargo Amarillo

RANGE: *Baja California, Mexico, to Panama; rarely to southern California.*

WHERE TO FISH: *Widely distributed in near-shore waters over rocky bottom, usually in 100 feet or less. Also roams into estuaries and even into freshwater rivers.*

DESCRIPTION: Nose and head are rosy, and most of the body is deep yellow or orange, as are the fins. A blue streak runs just below the eye.

SIZE: Average is 3-5 pounds; common to 10 or 12 pounds and occasionally hits 25 pounds or slightly more.

FOOD VALUE: Excellent.

GAME QUALITIES: Strong, bulldogging fight on light gear. Takes advantage of obstructions.

TACKLE: This is a fine casting fish for either spinning or revolving tackle, and even fly rods at times. Many are also caught, of course, on bottom-fishing gear.

LURES AND BAITS: For lures, topwater plugs and crankbaits are productive, especially in the rivers and channel edges. Jigs get the call for deep-dropping over the reefs. Sardines and other silvery baitfish are the most productive natural offerings.

Barred Pargo

Hoplopagrus guntheri

DESCRIPTION: Rounder in shape than most Snappers and with thick lips and stout dorsal spines. The belly is rusty red. Dark vertical bars make this one easy to spot.

SIZE: Most run 2-3 pounds, but some exceed 10 pounds.

FOOD VALUE: Very good.

GAME QUALITIES: A spirited fighter for its size, like most Snappers.

TACKLE: Spinning and baitcasting tackle will provide the best sport.

LURES AND BAITS: Mostly a night feeder, it can be caught during the day by bait-fishing on bottom or by bouncing jigs down deep. It likes Pilchards and similar silvery baitfishes and is also big on squid and shrimp.

OTHER NAMES:

Barred Snapper

RANGE: *Baja California, Mexico, and the Gulf of California to Panama.*

WHERE TO FISH: *Hard bottom in less than 100 feet of water. Common around some rocky points and shores.*

Blue-and-Gold Snapper

Lutjanus viridis

OTHER NAMES:

Pargo Rayado

RANGE: *Baja California, Mexico, and the Gulf of California to Panama.*

WHERE TO FISH: *Shallow rocky reefs in depths less than 100 feet.*

DESCRIPTION: The most brilliantly colored of the snappers, it has numerous bright blue stripes running horizontally over a gold background.

SIZE: Seldom exceed 12 inches.

FOOD VALUE: An excellent panfish.

GAME QUALITIES: Too small to rate highly.

TACKLE: Often seen by anglers but seldom targeted, it is generally easy to take on light spinning gear.

LURES AND BAITS: Small cutbaits of either fish or shellfish origin. Also hits small jigs, but seldom enthusiastically.

Colorado Snapper

Lutjanus colorado

DESCRIPTION: The body and fins are bright red and the belly is white. Faint dark bars sometimes show on smaller specimens. May also have a blue streak under the eye.

SIZE: Common at 2-10 pounds; sometimes reaches or surpasses 20 pounds. World record 20 pounds, 8 ounces.

FOOD VALUE: Excellent.

GAME QUALITIES: Very aggressive, especially in schools. Hits hard and dives fast, with strong resistance all the way.

TACKLE: This is a great casting target for spinning and baitcasting gear, also offering opportunistic shots for fly fishing. As with all Snappers, live-baiting and bottom fishing are also practiced with effect.

LURES AND BAITS: Noisy topwater plugs splashed around rocks in the surf zone will frequently bring a school of them to the surface, eager to strike. Unfortunately, the school may disappear just as quickly, so prompt response on the part of all anglers aboard is necessary, especially if the aim is to hook up on fly tackle. Besides surface plugs, they take spoons, jigs and swimming plugs. Very large poppers and streamers are the best flyrod choices. For bait fishing, nothing beats lively Sardines, although other baitfishes are acceptable and cut baits work fairly well.

OTHER NAMES:

**Red Snapper
Pargo Colorado**

RANGE: *Baja California, Mexico, to Panama; straggles to southern California.*

WHERE TO FISH: *Nearshore rock or reef areas and around emergent rocks along the coast; also in passes and river mouths.*

Jordan's Snapper

Lutjanus jordani

RANGE: Southern Mexico to Panama.

WHERE TO FISH: Around rocky shorelines and offshore islands, these fish frequently form large schools.

DESCRIPTION: Head more pointed than most Snappers. Upper back and top of head dark olive. Sides and belly purplish. Silvery spots form rows.

SIZE: Generally rather small, around a pound.

FOOD VALUE: Excellent.

GAME QUALITIES: Tough as other Snappers.

TACKLE: Seldom of much interest to anglers, who encounter them while fishing for bigger stuff.

LURES AND BAITS: Any available natural bait of appropriate size will do.

Mullet Snapper

Lutjanus aratus

OTHER NAMES:

Pargo Lisa

RANGE: Central Baja California, Mexico, to Panama.

WHERE TO FISH: It likes rock or reef bottom close to shore and is frequently caught around coastal rock outcroppings; also in bays. Sometimes taken in deeper water, to about 150 feet.

DESCRIPTION: With its long, slender body, it doesn't look much like most other Snappers. Color ranges from silvery red to almost yellow.

SIZE: In range of 3-6 pounds, but can grow quite large, sometimes 30. World record 33 pounds.

FOOD VALUE: Excellent.

GAME QUALITIES: A hard striker and fast runner.

TACKLE: Spinning and baitcasting are best for good sport.

LURES AND BAITS: Jigs, spoons and surface plugs are all good for random casting.

Pacific Cubera Snapper

Lutjanus novemfasciatus

DESCRIPTION: While "Pacific Cubera" is an obvious contradiction in terms ("Cubera" refers to Cuba), the closeness of this fish to the giant Cubera Snapper of tropical Atlantic waters is so obvious that the name has been widely adopted, even by the International Game Fish Association. The color of both species is brick red on the upper parts and lighter red on the sides, which are marked by dark vertical bars. Canine teeth are largest of all Snappers, but so is the rest of the fish!

SIZE: Common at 15-40 pounds and often runs heavier, to 50 or 75 pounds. Its Atlantic counterpart often exceeds 100 pounds and this one may get that big as well. World record 78 pounds, 12 ounces.

FOOD VALUE: Very good.

GAME QUALITIES: Considered the king of the Snappers on either light or heavy tackle. They wage a no-holds-barred fight.

TACKLE: Most sports angling takes one of two forms: trolling with ocean tackle and lines up to around 50-pound test, or casting with stout baitcasting rigs.

LURES AND BAITS: For trolling, large diving plugs get first call. For casting, the top choice is a big, cup-faced popping plug.

OTHER NAMES:

Pacific Dog Snapper

RANGE: *Northern Mexico to Panama.*

WHERE TO FISH: *Although some are caught in depths to at least 200 feet, they are far more frequently encountered by sportsmen near coastal rocks and outcroppings, and also in coastal streams, even ranging far into fresh water.*

Pacific Red Snapper

Lutjanus peru

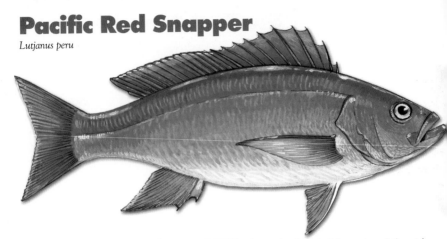

OTHER NAMES:

Huachinango

RANGE: *Baja California, Mexico, to Panama.*

WHERE TO FISH: *Deep rocky banks, up to about 120 feet, are its main habitat. Does not surface so readily as the Colorado.*

DESCRIPTION: Upper body is bright red and the sides are silvery red. Overall color is lighter than that of the Colorado Snapper, and it does not have the dark bars that are often apparent on the Colorado.

SIZE: Averages 3 or 4 pounds; tops out at perhaps 15 pounds. World record 12 pounds, 12 ounces.

FOOD VALUE: Excellent.

GAME QUALITIES: It is a strong, bulldogging fighter on reasonably light gear.

TACKLE: Stout bottom-fishing tackle is the most common, but if a concentration of Red Snapper can be found then deep-jigging with medium spinning or baitcasting gear is a blast.

LURES AND BAITS: For deep-jigging, leadhead jigs trimmed with hair or with hair-and-plastic combinations will get action. Natural baits are those that appeal to all the Snappers in its size class, mainly Pilchards and similar baitfishes, plus squid.

Spotted Rose Snapper

Lutjanus guttatus

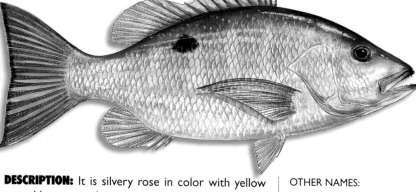

DESCRIPTION: It is silvery rose in color with yellow or gold tones and a prominent black spot on the upper rear side and blue spots on the head.

SIZE: Usually small, it averages only a pound or 2, but often reaches 4 pounds and sometimes tops 10.

FOOD VALUE: Excellent.

GAME QUALITIES: It hits hard and wages a throbbing, diving fight.

TACKLE: Light spinning and baitcasting gear are the best matches for this one.

LURES AND BAITS: Very aggressive, it hits jigs avidly and will take many kinds of naturals, topped by Pilchards and other silvery baitfish.

OTHER NAMES:

Rose Snapper

RANGE: *Gulf of California to Panama.*

WHERE TO FISH: *Seems to like both sandy and rocky bottoms of nearshore areas, and also roams bays and estuaries. It's a favorite of shorebound fishermen in many areas, as well as anglers in boats.*

To most sport fishermen, a Snook is a Snook is a Snook and a big Snook rates as one of the most coveted of light-tackle prizes. "Big" is the key word here. There actually are several types of snook in tropical Pacific waters (to say nothing of several entirely different ones in the Atlantic), but only two reach trophy size. Maybe we should make that just one, since they are so nearly alike that few anglers care to, or try to, distinguish between them, and neither does the International Game Fish Association. Classic casting for Snook takes place along the shorelines of tidal streams from Mexico through Panama, but the fishing is frequently more productive around inlets and river mouths, or in the surf. The several smaller varieties of Snook all wear the same vivid black lateral stripe as their big relatives, and they also strike many of the same baits and lures, but anglers view them mainly as curiosities, or even nuisances. One minor exception is the Bigeye Snook, which does get large enough to provide good sport on light casting or spinning tackle even if it doesn't offer much in the way of bragging material.

The Snooks

Black Snook

White Snook

Little Snook

Longspine Snook

Bigeye Snook

Humpback Snook

Black Snook/White Snook

Centropomus nigrescens/viridis

OTHER NAMES:

Robalo

RANGE: *Baja California, Mexico, and the Gulf of California to Panama.*

WHERE TO FISH: *Usually found in or near coastal streams and mangrove estuaries. Sometimes they run far into fresh water. Also found in channels through flats, and in the surf zone, especially near inlets and river mouths.*

DESCRIPTION: These two giants of the Pacific Snook clan are treated here as one entry because, from an angler's point of view, there is no difference (or between them and the Atlantic Common Snook for that matter). In appearance, habits, range and size the Black and White Snook are identical, and only by studying fin structure and gill rakers can they be distinguished. If an angler is interested in separating them, the quickest point of comparison is the third dorsal spine. On the Black Snook that spine is shorter than the fourth spine; on the White Snook it is longer.

SIZE: Most range from 5-20 pounds; catches over 50 pounds if not likely are always possible. At this writing, the largest Snook in sporting records is a 57-pound Black Snook.

FOOD VALUE: Smaller fish excellent; big ones good.

GAME QUALITIES: One of the storied shallow-water gamesters and well deserving of its reputation for powerful runs and spectacular jumps.

TACKLE: Baitcasting tackle is the first choice, with spinning a close runner-up. Light classes of ocean trolling tackle also have a strong niche, as well as fly.

LURES AND BAITS: Surface plugs, swimming plugs and spoons are leading choices for shoreline casting, but leadhead jigs retrieved slowly along the bottom will usually drum up more action. Outsize poppers and long streamers are favored by flyrod anglers. Small baitfish, shrimp and crabs are proven producers.

Little Snook/Longspine Snook

Centropomus robalito/armatus

DESCRIPTION: Here's another pair of closely similar snook that are common enough catches although too small to generate much interest in distinguishing between them—at least among anglers. The prominent feature they have in common is a sword-like second spine of the anal fin, so long that it reaches to or beyond the beginning of the tail fin when depressed. Both are silvery in color with thin black lateral lines. Again, it takes a count of fin rays and gill rakers to make a certain identification, although robalito is a bit thinner of body.

SIZE: Seldom longer than a foot; maximum possibly 18 inches.

FOOD VALUE: Excellent but seldom killed by sportsmen.

GAME QUALITIES: Spunky and aerial-minded, it is not large enough to resist with any kind of authority.

TACKLE: Fun on the lightest spinning and fly gear.

LURES AND BAITS: Small jigs and spoons; streamer or hair flies about an inch long.

OTHER NAMES:

Robalito
Swordfin Snook
Armed Snook

RANGE: *Baja California, Mexico, to Panama.*

WHERE TO FISH: *Shallow estuaries and coastal streams.*

Bigeye Snook

Centropomus medius

OTHER NAMES:

Popeyed Snook
Blackfin Snook

RANGE: *Southern Baja California, Mexico, and southern Gulf of California to Panama.*

WHERE TO FISH: *Estuaries and river mouths.*

DESCRIPTION: Like all Snook, this one is silvery with a black lateral line. The fins are dusky. Its large eye usually calls quick attention to its identification, besides which, it is the only Pacific Snook other than the Black and White big boys that grows to a fair size.

SIZE: Averages perhaps 2-4 pounds; occasionally hits 5 or 6 pounds.

FOOD VALUE: Excellent.

GAME QUALITIES: Quite tough for its size and an excellent jumper. A fine foe on light casting equipment.

TACKLE: Spinning and baitcasting are the most consistent producers. Fly gear is useful in certain situations, such as a creek mouth at falling tide where action is obvious.

LURES AND BAITS: Small jigs and spoons lead the pack. Crankbaits are good too. Small streamers, to about 2 inches long, tied with shiny or bright-colored material, make good ammunition for fly casters.

Humpback Snook

Centropomus unionensis

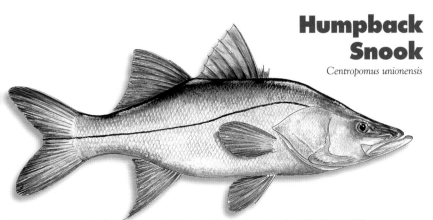

DESCRIPTION: Looks very much like the Little Snook and Longspine Snook, except that the stout second spine of the anal fin is short, not reaching the tail fin. The lateral line is pale and the fins are yellowish.

SIZE: Runs no larger than 12-18 inches.

FOOD VALUE: Excellent but seldom kept by sportsmen.

GAME QUALITIES: Spunky and aerial-minded, it is not large enough to resist with any kind of authority.

TACKLE: Fun on the lightest spinning and fly gear.

LURES AND BAITS: Small jigs and spoons; streamer or hair flies about an inch long.

OTHER NAMES:

Union Snook

RANGE: El Salvador to Panama.

WHERE TO FISH: Freshwater streams, estuaries and protected bays.

I n the sportfishing world, Shark reviews have long been mixed, with a few species gaining high praise as gamefish, and many others looked upon as time-wasting nuisances. The biggest difference, naturally, is size, and when it comes to size, the Shark family has it in spades. The Great White Shark is the largest predatory fish in the ocean, and several other kinds often weigh half a ton or more. In any size, however, Sharks are generally strong and speedy fighters, and some of them get off spectacular jumps. More than that, large Sharks are widely available to nearly every angler, regardless of where they fish or the sophistication of their tackle. For this reason they are sometimes referred to as the "poor man's marlin." Sharks in journalism and literature are usually presented as evil man-eaters. Some are, of course, particularly the Great White—well, not evil, really, but certainly a threat to human life in certain circumstances. Actually, however, it is mostly the other way around. Sharks have become so much in demand as human food that the future of many species is threatened.

The Sharks

Angel Shark
Blacktip Shark
Blue Shark
Bonnethead
Bull Shark
Common Thresher
Dusky Shark
Galapagos Shark
Gray Smoothhound
Great Hammerhead
Lemon Shark
Leopard Shark
Nurse Shark
Oceanic Whitetip Shark
Pacific Sharpnose Shark
Salmon Shark
Scalloped Hammerhead
Shortfin Mako
Silky Shark
Smooth Hammerhead
Soupfin Shark
Spiny Dogfish
Tiger Shark
White Shark
Whitenose Shark

Angel Shark

Squatina californica

OTHER NAMES:

Pacific Angel Shark
Tiburon Angel

RANGE: *Alaska to the Gulf of California, Mexico; also Costa Rica, Panama and Chile.*

WHERE TO FISH: *On sand and mud bottoms virtually anywhere from close inshore to at least 500 feet deep.*

DESCRIPTION: This strange fish is sort of a cross between Sharks and Rays and is not classified with either side but in a separate biological order. Its body is flattened like that of a Ray and the coloration on top is reddish brown to dark gray with scattered darker spots. The underside is white. Although it may look rather harmless compared to most Sharks it has sharp teeth and an aggressive nature and can deliver a serious bite to a careless diver or angler.

SIZE: May reach about 50 pounds but the majority of catches run about 10-30 pounds.

FOOD VALUE: Very good; commercial value has caused a decline in numbers.

GAME QUALITIES: Deemed rather sluggish on the end of a line, but still a respectable battler on reasonably light gear.

TACKLE: Seldom targeted. Most sportsmen are inclined to look at it as a nuisance or an interloper. Most are caught accidentally on boat tackle—live bait outfits, especially—and a few from shore on heavy spinning gear or surf tackle.

LURES AND BAITS: It lives by ambushing live fish from a buried position in soft bottom, so live baits are obviously the best, and the species of bait matters little. Dead baits and cut baits are also accepted.

Blacktip Shark

Carcharhinus limbatus

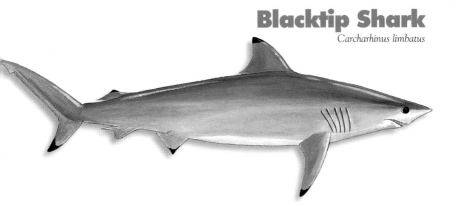

DESCRIPTION: Tips of the dorsal and pectoral fins are black, as is the lower lobe of the caudal fin. It has a short snout and stout body, and the dorsal begins at a point above the rear portion of the pectoral fin. Color is gray above, white below, usually with a distinct line of division.

SIZE: Common from 5-30 pounds, not many Blacktips reach 100 pounds, but the potential is to 200 or more. World record 270 pounds, 9 ounces.

FOOD VALUE: Very good.

GAME QUALITIES: Pound for pound, probably the scrappiest of small sharks. Wages a wild battle on light tackle, marked by long runs and frantic jumps, especially in shallow water.

TACKLE AND BAITS: Spinning, baitcasting and even fly casting are popular among many anglers.

LURES AND BAITS: Blacktips will hit a variety of artificial lures, especially topwater plugs and flyrod poppers, streamer flies, slow-swimming jigs and underwater plugs. They also eagerly take any small live baitfish or fresh cut bait, plus shrimp and squid.

OTHER NAMES:

Spinner Shark Volador

RANGE: *Baja California, Mexico, to Peru.*

WHERE TO FISH: *Found anywhere from the deep sea to shorelines and bays. One of the most familiar inshore sharks, it is often seen on shallow flats and along beaches and shorelines.*

Blue Shark

Prionace glauca

OTHER NAMES:

Blue Dogfish
Blue Whaler
Mano

RANGE: *Alaska to Panama.*

WHERE TO FISH: *Offshore. Commonly found near the surface in colder waters, but usually stays very deep in warm seas.*

DESCRIPTION: Bright blue color, pointed snout and extra-long dorsal fins make this shark easy to pick out. Underside is white.

SIZE: Averages 100-300 pounds; seldom tops 500, although the maximum may be much larger. World record 528 pounds.

FOOD VALUE: Fair.

GAME QUALITIES: It's only a so-so fighter compared to some other Sharks and is considered a pest by most offshore anglers, but it does nevertheless offer a challenge to those who fish for it with light tackle.

TACKLE: Light ocean outfits with lines testing 20 or 30 pounds are the best choices for fun.

LURES AND BAITS: Blue Sharks are most easily hooked by chumming with whole or cut fish and baiting with the same.

Bonnethead

Sphyrna tiburo

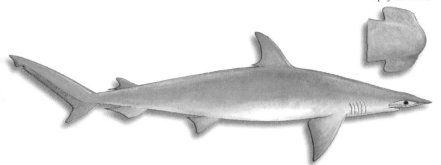

DESCRIPTION: It's one of the Hammerheads but the head is rounded or shovel-shaped, rather than widely elongated as with the larger members of the group. The color is usually a very light gray, appearing almost white in the water.

SIZE: Averages 2-5 pounds; occasionally tops 10 pounds and can reach 20 or so. World record 23 pounds, 11 ounces.

FOOD VALUE: Good.

GAME QUALITIES: Fight on light tackle is wild but brief.

TACKLE: Light spinning and baitcasting outfits.

LURES AND BAITS: Although Bonnetheads feed mostly on shellfish, they will take small dead fish or cut fish, as well as shrimp or squid.

OTHER NAMES:

Shovelnose Shark

RANGE: *Southern California to Panama.*

WHERE TO FISH: *Found mostly inshore and in estuaries, usually roaming shallow flats.*

Bull Shark

Carcharhinus leucas

OTHER NAMES:

Freshwater Shark
Gambu

RANGE: *Baja California, Mexico, to Panama; also Hawaii and, occasionally, southern California.*

WHERE TO FISH: *Inhabits both offshore and nearshore waters and sometimes roams far into freshwater streams.*

DESCRIPTION: The snout is short and wide. The first dorsal fin is large and starts above the middle of the pectoral fin. The second dorsal is much smaller. Color is dingy black or gray above and white below.

SIZE: Can exceed 10 feet and 400 pounds, but most run 6-8 feet and 100-300 pounds. World record 697 pounds, 12 ounces.

FOOD VALUE: Good.

GAME QUALITIES: A rugged fighter; strong and persevering.

TACKLE: Although more appropriately matched to medium ocean outfits, the Bull is one of the pet targets of adventurous spin, plug and fly casters when it can be fished on rather shallow flats.

LURES AND BAITS: It will take a variety of dead fish and can also be chummed into a mood for hitting artificial lures, including topwater plugs and large streamer flies or flyrod poppers.

Common Thresher

Alopias vulpinus

DESCRIPTION: The long, scythe-like tail (which it uses to stun schooling baitfish) is a dead giveaway. A similar species, the Bigeye Thresher (*Alopias superciliosus*) is distinguished by its unmistakably huge eye.

SIZE: Average is 250-350 pounds; both species grow to perhaps 1,000 pounds. World record 767 pounds, 3 ounces.

FOOD VALUE: Excellent, one of the best Sharks for the table.

GAME QUALITIES: A fine fighter, deserving of big-game status.

TACKLE: Heavy classes of ocean trolling or standup tackle. Most are caught by deep-drifting, but occasionally they may be taken by trolling or visual baiting.

LURES AND BAITS: Small live fish of schooling varieties, such as Herring and Mackerel, make the best baits.

OTHER NAMES:

Thresher Shark

RANGE: *Southern California to Panama.*

WHERE TO FISH: *Usually the deep sea. It is sometimes encountered at the surface but generally is caught deep, especially the Bigeye Thresher, which only comes near the surface at night.*

Dusky Shark

Carcharhinus obscurus

OTHER NAMES:

Ground Shark
Bay Shark

RANGE: *Baja California, Mexico, and the Gulf of California to Panama.*

WHERE TO FISH: *Primarily coastal, from beaches to the edge of the continental shelf.*

DESCRIPTION: It can be distinguished from similar species such as the Sandbar Shark by a ridge between the dorsal fins. The usual color is dark gray above, shading to whitish below. The head is short and pointed, the dorsal fin triangular.

SIZE: Most catches are 8 or 10 feet long, with weights up to 250 pounds. Maximum is probably around 500 pounds. World record 764 pounds.

FOOD VALUE: Good.

GAME QUALITIES: A good fighter, but not ranked with the Mako for gameness.

TACKLE: Medium to heavy ocean or standup outfits. Lighter gear can be used at your own risk.

LURES AND BAITS: Any sort of fresh dead fish or large fresh chunk of cutbait will probably draw attention.

Galapagos Shark

Carcharhinus galapagensis

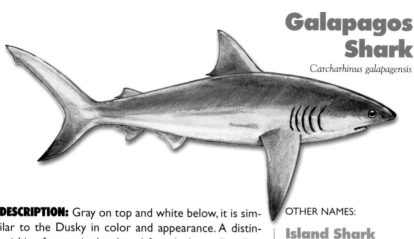

DESCRIPTION: Gray on top and white below, it is similar to the Dusky in color and appearance. A distinguishing feature is the dorsal fin, which is taller than that of the Dusky.

SIZE: To 200 pounds. Record 188 pounds, 6 ounces.

FOOD VALUE: Good.

GAME QUALITIES: Fights well and with long runs.

TACKLE: Ocean tackle in the 20- to 30-pound range.

LURES AND BAITS: Live or dead fish, or squid.

OTHER NAMES:

Island Shark

RANGE: *Baja California, Mexico, to Panama.*

WHERE TO FISH: *Most often observed around offshore islands, but also seen along the edge of the continental shelf.*

Gray Smoothhound

Mustelus californicus

DESCRIPTION: Body is slender and nose pointed. Color gray above with white underparts. Teeth are blunt. The similar Brown Smoothhound runs smaller.

SIZE: Usually is less than 3 feet long.

FOOD VALUE: Very good.

GAME QUALITIES: Spirited fighter on light gear.

TACKLE: Various kinds of light inshore gear.

LURES AND BAITS: Often spooky about biting, it is more easily coaxed to squid, shrimp or crab than to baitfishes.

RANGE: *Northern California to and including the Gulf of California, Mexico.*

WHERE TO FISH: *Very common inshore over shallow mud and sand bottoms, but occasionally taken at 100 feet of so.*

Great Hammerhead

Sphyrna mokarran

OTHER NAMES:

Giant Hammerhead
Mano Kihi Kihi

RANGE: *Baja California, Mexico, and the Gulf of California to Panama.*

WHERE TO FISH: *Most commonly seen around the edge of the continental shelf in around 200-300 feet of water. It also ventures close to shore, but seldom far to sea.*

DESCRIPTION: If this huge fellow cannot be distinguished from other Hammerheads by size alone, note that the frontal edge of its "hammer" is not rounded, but flat. Also, it is the only Hammerhead in which the rear edge of the pelvic fin is curved.

SIZE: Many specimens exceed 500 pounds and some reach twice that weight. Maximum could be as much as one ton. World record 991 pounds.

FOOD VALUE: Good.

GAME QUALITIES: Its huge size is its best weapon; strong but not spectacular.

TACKLE: Only the heaviest sporting gear stands much of a chance—130-pound line or, at the least, 80-pound.

LURES AND BAITS: Will take large fresh-dead baitfish, but is more easily hooked on oversize live baits, especially Yellowtail or Bonito.

Lemon Shark

Negaprion brevirostris

DESCRIPTION: Color is light brown to yellow with a yellowish cast to the underside. The first dorsal fin is short and not much larger than the second dorsal. The pectorals are triangular and wide.

SIZE: Commonly seen in many sizes, from around 20 pounds to well over 100 pounds. Maximum is around 10 feet and 400 pounds. World record 405 pounds.

FOOD VALUE: Good.

GAME QUALITIES: It is not a jumper like the Blacktip, but is a strong fighter and a good foe on light to medium tackle.

TACKLE: Spinning, baitcasting and fly outfits can often be employed in shallow water, but the most practical choice is light to medium ocean tackle.

LURES AND BAITS: The Lemon will take a variety of natural baits, both fish and shellfish, and also artificial lures that are carefully and properly presented.

OTHER NAMES:

Yellow Shark
Brown Shark

RANGE: *Baja California, Mexico, and the Gulf of California to Panama.*

WHERE TO FISH: *Seldom roams far offshore but does most of its feeding in the shallows, sometimes on flats, but also in deeper bay waters, channels and river mouths.*

Leopard Shark

Triakis semifasciata

RANGE: *Oregon to Baja California, Mexico, and the northern Gulf of California.*

WHERE TO FISH: *Likes both rocky and soft-bottom flats, usually shallow and near shore, but is noted from offshore waters as well.*

DESCRIPTION: Color is gray above and white below, with numerous large patches and spots on the back, sides and tail. The nose is short and blunt.

SIZE: Usually runs 10-20 pounds but is sometimes caught to 40 pounds and is said to reach 75 or more. World record 40 pounds, 10 ounces.

FOOD VALUE: Very good.

GAME QUALITIES: A very active opponent on light tackle.

TACKLE: Spinning is ideal; baitcasting and Salmon gear are also sporty.

LURES AND BAITS: Small schooling baitfishes such as Herring, plus squid, shrimp or crab top the list. Lures seldom gain their approval.

Nurse Shark

Ginglymostoma cirratum

DESCRIPTION: The color is brown or deep rust. Strong distinguishing features include its very small, underslung mouth and barbels at the nostrils.

SIZE: In shallow water, most run from 5 to 50 pounds, but they can grow quite large in deeper water—to at least 10 or 12 feet and several hundred pounds. World record 241 pounds, 9 ounces.

FOOD VALUE: Excellent.

GAME QUALITIES: Very sluggish and probably the worst fighter of all the Sharks.

TACKLE: In shallow water, even the lightest kinds of tackle will easily handle a Nurse Shark, so take your choice. In deep water, heavy spinning and light ocean tackle will handle even the biggest ones you're likely to hook, because they are mostly dead weight.

LURES AND BAITS: Although its natural diet is shellfish, Nurse Sharks eagerly take cut fish. They are not great candidates for active live baits or artificial lures.

RANGE: *Gulf of California, Mexico, to Panama.*

WHERE TO FISH: *Frequently sighted on shallow flats where it usually is lying still. Also lies still in deeper water under reef and rock ledges, and around navigation markers.*

Oceanic Whitetip Shark

Carcharhinus longimanus

RANGE: *Southern California to Panama; also Hawaii.*

WHERE TO FISH: *Sticks almost entirely to the deep blue or the edge of the continental shelf.*

DESCRIPTION: Easily spotted by the glaring white tips of the dorsal, pectoral and caudal fins. Even without the white (and it's absent on a rare specimen) the high, rounded dorsal and long, rounded pectoral fins are giveaways.

SIZE: Up to 8-10 feet and 100-150 pounds. World record 369 pounds.

FOOD VALUE: Good.

GAME QUALITIES: An excellent battler on light tackle, but easy to handle on heavy gear.

TACKLE: Light to medium ocean or standup tackle, with lines to 30-pound test.

LURES AND BAITS: It often is a picky biter that insists on live bait, such as Mackerel, small Jacks or small Bonito, although it has been taken on a variety of cut-baits.

Pacific Sharpnose Shark

Rhizoprionodon longurio

DESCRIPTION: This is a slender gray Shark with a long, pointed snout.

SIZE: Averages only 2 or 3 feet long.

FOOD VALUE: Good.

GAME QUALITIES: Zippy and strong fighter.

TACKLE: Spinning and baitcasting.

LURES AND BAITS: Eats most any small fish, plus squid and crab. Takes artificials only rarely.

RANGE: *Lower Baja California, Mexico, to Panama.*

WHERE TO FISH: *Very common inshore, especially in the Gulf of California. May strike anywhere from the surf or shoreline out to 100 feet.*

Salmon Shark

Lamna ditropis

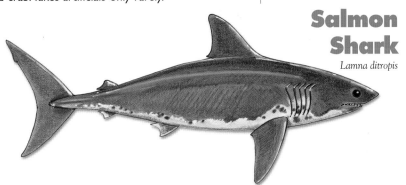

DESCRIPTION: First dorsal fin is high and uniformly dark. Top color is blue or gray, often mottled. The underside is white with dusky blotches.

SIZE: Reported to 10 feet and nearly 400 pounds.

FOOD VALUE: Good but numbers are declining.

GAME QUALITIES: A strong and persevering battler that will test most tackle.

TACKLE: Heavy Salmon tackle or light-to-medium ocean gear.

LURES AND BAITS: Although its diet includes bottom fishes, it feeds largely on Salmon, and so a chunk of Salmon always is a dependable offering.

OTHER NAMES:

Mackerel Shark

RANGE: *Alaska to southern California.*

WHERE TO FISH: *Often caught close to shore, but roams far offshore as well.*

Scalloped Hammerhead

Sphyrna lewini

RANGE: *Baja California, Mexico, and Gulf of California to Panama; also common off Hawaii.*

WHERE TO FISH: *Open ocean, but commonly roams close to the beaches and sometimes into large bays.*

DESCRIPTION: Light brown above, shading to white on underside. Pectoral fin has a dark tip, but on underside only. Front edge of "hammer" is slightly rounded, with several indentations, including one in center.

SIZE: Averages about 75-175 pounds; can exceed 200 pounds. World record 335 pounds, 15 ounces.

FOOD VALUE: Good.

GAME QUALITIES: A willing feeder that's usually easy to hook. Runs are fast and strong.

TACKLE: Since it is a middleweight among sharks, it makes a good candidate for light to medium tackle. Heavy spinning outfits, as well as saltwater outfits with lines up to 30-pound test, make good matchups.

LURES AND BAITS: Live or fresh-dead baitfish will be the most eagerly accepted.

Shortfin Mako

Isurus oxyrinchus

DESCRIPTION: While not so bright as the Blue Shark, the Makos are blue above and white below. They have bulging teeth which differ from those of other well-known sharks in being long, narrow and pointed, rather than v-shaped. A similar species, the Longfin Mako (*I. paucus*) is only rarely caught. The "Longfin" label refers more to the very long pectorals than to the dorsal, although that fin also stands higher. The caudal fins of both are relatively small and crescent-shaped.

SIZE: Usual range is 200-600 pounds, but both species attain weights of more than 1,000 pounds. World record 1,221 pounds.

FOOD VALUE: Excellent.

GAME QUALITIES: Considered by many big-game anglers as deserving of rank among the big Billfishes. A very strong and vicious fighter that often gets off high, spectacular leaps.

TACKLE AND BAITS: Best to choose ocean tackle, in at least the 30-pound line class, with 50-pound and 80-pound lines needed to handle the big ones. Unfortunately, it's difficult to pick the size, so heavier stuff is always a wise idea in Mako territory—which, for practical purposes, can be considered the same as Blue Marlin territory. Usually will strike rigged baits, such as Mullet and Mackerel, but a live Bonito or similar baitfish is better, if available.

OTHER NAMES:

Bonito Shark
Blue Pointer
Mano

RANGE: *Southern California to Panama.*

WHERE TO FISH: *The open sea. Shortfin Makos frequently cruise, and strike at, the surface, whereas the Longfin is almost entirely a deep dweller.*

Silky Shark

Carcharhinus falciformis

RANGE: *Southern Baja California, Mexico, to Panama.*

WHERE TO FISH: *Prefers the continental shelf, but roams far to sea.*

DESCRIPTION: Rather slender and snout is short. Color silky brown to blue above, white below.

SIZE: Usually 30-100 pounds—but is not rare at 200-300.

FOOD VALUE: Good.

GAME QUALITIES: Very rugged on suitable tackle.

TACKLE: The Silky can often be sighted and baited in clear offshore waters. Light classes of ocean tackle, plus heavy spinning and baitcasting gear, will give good sport on smaller fish that the angler can select.

LURES AND BAITS: Baits cut from fresh-dead fish.

Smooth Hammerhead

Sphyrna zygaena

RANGE: *Central California to the northern Gulf of California, Mexico.*

WHERE TO FISH: *Roams the open sea, with occasional forays into shallower water. Commonly seen at the surface by offshore anglers.*

DESCRIPTION: Size and habits similar to the Scalloped Hammerhead, and few anglers make any distinction.

SIZE: Averages around 100 pounds. World record 363.

FOOD VALUE: Good.

GAME QUALITIES: Fast and strong.

TACKLE: Like the Scalloped Hammerhead, it is a good candidate for lighter tackle.

LURES AND BAITS: Although it usually will take a live or dead fish presented to it by sight at the surface, its extensive appetite seems to favor Skates and Rays.

Soupfin Shark

Galeorhinus zyopterus

DESCRIPTION: The nose is long and pointed and the eye oval-shaped. Color is blue or gray above, white on the underparts. Dorsal and caudal fins are black-tipped, with a white spot on the dorsal.

SIZE: A rather small Shark, it averages around 10 to 30 pounds. Maximum is around 90 pounds.

FOOD VALUE: Good.

GAME QUALITIES: Mediocre, due to relatively small size and rather sluggish nature.

TACKLE: Can be caught on rather light gear, including Salmon tackle and heavy spinning.

LURES AND BAITS: Not generally selective, but squid is probably the best choice of bait. Also eats numerous kinds of fish and cut baits.

OTHER NAMES:

Tope Shark

RANGE: *Alaska to upper Baja California, Mexico.*

WHERE TO FISH: *Wanders from offshore to shallow bays.*

Spiny Dogfish
Squalus acanthias

OTHER NAMES:

Pike Shark
Grayfish

RANGE: *Alaska to northern Baja California, Mexico.*

WHERE TO FISH: *Usually travels in schools and is found close inshore in cold water, going progressively deeper near the southern end of its range. It roams from the bottom to the surface.*

DESCRIPTION: Dogfish are brownish gray above, light gray below, with scattered light spots on the sides. The snout is long and flat. The second dorsal fin is smaller than the first dorsal, but each is fitted with a sharp spike on the forward edge that can administer a painful stab to the incautious angler.

SIZE: Averages 2 or 3 feet; seldom exceeds four feet. World record 15 pounds, 2 ounces.

FOOD VALUE: Very good; in Britain it is the usual "fish" in fish and chips.

GAME QUALITIES: Poor. Mostly considered a nuisance by inshore or nearshore anglers and deepwater fishermen alike.

TACKLE: Sporty only on light gear, such as spinning and baitcasting outfits.

LURES AND BAITS: To the dismay of most fishermen it hits a wide variety of fish and shellfish baits, live or dead.

Tiger Shark

Galeocerdo cuvier

DESCRIPTION: The color is dark above, yellowish below, usually with numerous dark markings. On smaller specimens, these markings take the shape of spots—hence the name "Leopard," that is sometimes erroneously applied. The big ones become "Tigers" as the spots grow and blend together into stripes. The patterns, however, do vary a great deal, with both stripes and spots present on many specimens, and markings nearly absent on some very large ones.

SIZE: This is one of the largest Sharks likely to be encountered by coastal anglers. Quite a few 1,000-pounders have been taken—some from surf and piers—and the potential is to more than a ton. Most sporting catches run from less than 100 pounds to 600 or so. World record 1,780 pounds.

FOOD VALUE: Small ones are very good.

GAME QUALITIES: Not spectacular but its size and strength always create a great challenge for the angler.

TACKLE: Only the stoutest ocean or standup tackle will suffice for adult fish. But, of course, many small Tigers have fallen to surf tackle and to heavy baitcasting or spinning gear.

LURES AND BAITS: Although the Tiger Shark will eat virtually anything, including shellfish, mammal, and tin cans, some particularly good baits are Ray or Skate wings and live or dead fish. Baits must be appropriate to the size class of the Sharks being sought. This means very big baits indeed if you're after a monster. Tigers don't often strike artificials, but once in a while will hit trolled lures, especially if rigged in combination with a strip or other natural bait.

OTHER NAMES:

Leopard Shark
Mano

RANGE: *Southern California to Panama; also Hawaii.*

WHERE TO FISH: *Tigers like to stay near the coast, occasionally wandering fairly far offshore, but not a denizen of the open sea. They are encountered in the surf and in bays, as well as over reefs and outside rocks.*

White Shark

Carcharadon carcharias

OTHER NAMES:

Great White Shark
White Pointer
Maneater
Niuchi

RANGE: *Not common anywhere, it prefers temperate waters and on our coast is most likely to be encountered from southern Alaska to southern California. Its range, however, does extend to Panama and also Hawaii.*

WHERE TO FISH: *The open sea, although it frequently ventures near the beaches, and rarely even into coastal streams.*

DESCRIPTION: The body is thick and bulky with a large caudal keel. It usually looks lighter in the water than other big sharks, although the actual color varies from gray to light brown above and white below. The nose is pointed, the teeth triangular and serrated. A black patch may be present at base of pectoral fin.

SIZE: This is the largest of all predatory Sharks and has been recorded to as much as 20 feet and 2 tons, but it is not common enough anywhere to state an average size. Anglers have taken them from less than 200 pounds to more than 2,000. World record 2,664 pounds.

FOOD VALUE: Smaller ones are good but seldom eaten; with big ones it could be the other way around.

GAME QUALITIES: Size and rarity alone place it among the ultimate angling challenges.

TACKLE: Only the heaviest sporting tackle available makes sense when going after huge Sharks, particularly this species.

LURES AND BAITS: Live fish, such as Tuna, Dolphin or Bonito, as large as can be handled by angler and crew, may attract the quarry from longer distances, but the same baits fished dead are also fine. Large chunks of any kind of flesh are also good, but note that sporting rules prohibit the use of mammals or mammal parts for bait or chum. Great Whites respond to heavy and continued chumming, and most encounters are probably the result of this tactic.

Whitenose Shark

Nasolamia velox

DESCRIPTION: Color is gray to brownish gray above, white below. Its name comes from a black spot outlined in white on the upper tip of its nose.

SIZE: Usually runs 30-100 pounds but can push 200 pounds.

FOOD VALUE: Good.

GAME QUALITIES: Strong, but the fight is neither showy nor long-lasting.

TACKLE: Light ocean tackle with 20- to 40-pound test both adequate to the job and sporting.

LURES AND BAITS: Small live fish are the best, but squid, crab and cut fish are also accepted.

RANGE: *Gulf of California to Panama.*

WHERE TO FISH: *They are not often seen in water shallower than about 50 feet, but from there to about 200 feet, they may hit anywhere from top to bottom.*

All the fish in this chapter are cousins to the Sharks, and can be found in virtually every Pacific habitat from the deep sea to far up coastal rivers. For the most part, fishermen try to avoid them but that's not easy to do, especially for anglers who fish natural baits on the bottom. Rays and Skates do pull hard for a short while and are adept at plastering their wide bodies to the bottom to resist lifting, but they are nearly always a disappointment to their captors, who are expecting to pull up something a bit more glamorous, only to have an ugly Ray or Skate come into view. What's worse, some of these critters are dangerous, in particular the Stingray, whose stab is not only excruciatingly painful but, without proper treatment, potentially deadly as well. Wading anglers are the ones primarily susceptible to Stingray damage, but boaters must take care also. Best to cut the line if you hook one. The species covered in this chapter all might bite an angler's bait. Large, free-roaming swimmers, such as the Manta and Eagle Rays are familiar but not included here because they rarely end up on a line except by accidental snagging.

Rays and Relatives

Big Skate

California Skate

Shovelnose Guitarfish

Pacific Electric Ray

Round Stingray

Largetooth Sawfish

Big Skate

Raja binoculata

RANGE: *Alaska to northern Baja California, Mexico, and the Gulf of California.*

WHERE TO FISH: *Not targeted, it is an incidental catch, usually from shallow inshore waters, but from well offshore as well.*

DESCRIPTION: Large ocelli—eye-like spots—in the middle of each wing are giveaways to the identify of this big fellow, the largest of the skates. Top color is brown to gray and the underside white.

SIZE: Known to reach 8 feet in span and to weigh at least 200 pounds, it is common at about 20-50 pounds. World record 91 pounds.

FOOD VALUE: "Wings" are very good but are usually shunned by anglers.

GAME QUALITIES: A tough customer, it can make long and fairly fast runs, besides which it is very difficult to pull from the bottom.

TACKLE: None specific to the task. Nearly always caught unintentionally.

LURES AND BAITS: Eats mostly shellfish but is a scavenger and will take dead baitfish and cut baits as well.

California Skate

Raja inornata

DESCRIPTION: Top color is brown or olive, with rather vague mottling, and the underside dingy yellow. The nose is sharply pointed and there are prominent twin claspers at the rear of the body.

SIZE: Averages 1-2 feet in span.

FOOD VALUE: Very good, but mostly shunned by anglers.

GAME QUALITIES: Poor.

TACKLE: None specific to the task. Nearly always caught unintentionally.

LURES AND BAITS: Eats mostly shellfish but is a scavenger and will take dead baitfish and cut baits as well.

RANGE: Alaska to central Baja California, Mexico.

WHERE TO FISH: If you bottom-fish, they may pester you anywhere from inshore baits to offshore banks.

Shovelnose Guitarfish

Rhinobatos productus

OTHER NAMES:

Shovelnose
Pez Guitarra

RANGE: *Central California to Baja California, Mexico, and the Gulf of California.*

WHERE TO FISH: *Rarely targeted, they are taken mostly from soft bottom near shore.*

DESCRIPTION: Color is solid—brown above and dingy white below. Head is long and shovel-shaped.

SIZE: Three-foot specimens common. Some exceed 5 feet and 40 pounds. World record 21 pounds, 8 ounces.

FOOD VALUE: Fillets from the saddle are good.

GAME QUALITIES: Poor.

TACKLE: Usually caught on gear chosen for other species.

LURES AND BAITS: Prefers clams and crabs but will take cut fish.

Pacific Electric Ray

Torpedo californica

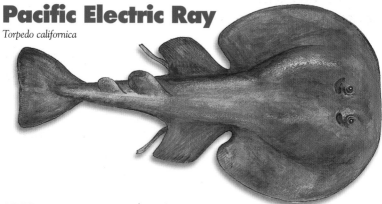

OTHER NAMES:

Torpedo
Torpedo Ray

RANGE: *Northern British Columbia, Canada, to Central Baja California, Mexico.*

WHERE TO FISH: *Anglers prefer to know where not to fish, but it could show up from near shore to 500 feet or more of water. Prefers sand bottom near rocks.*

DESCRIPTION: Nearly round in shape and, unlike most other Rays and Skates, it has a wide caudal fin.

SIZE: From a couple of feet to more than 3 feet.

FOOD VALUE: Poor.

GAME QUALITIES: Poor.

TACKLE: Not targeted. It isn't extremely dangerous, but can administer a severe shock, so take care when you catch one.

LURES AND BAITS: Feeds on Herrings and other small fish that it stuns while hovering above them. It can suspend itself virtually motionless.

Round Stingray

Urolophus halleri

DESCRIPTION: Most common of Stingrays. All must be viewed with the same leery eye.

SIZE: Usually a foot or so, but record is 185 pounds.

FOOD VALUE: Wings are good, but usually shunned.

GAME QUALITIES: Can cling stubbornly to the bottom.

TACKLE: Usually taken on light inshore gear.

LURES AND BAITS: Any sort of shellfish plus cut fish.

OTHER NAMES:

Raya de Espina

RANGE: *Northern California to Panama; similar species in Hawaii.*

WHERE TO FISH: *All too common on sand or mud bottom, often along beaches and in shallow bays.*

Largetooth Sawfish

Pristis pristis

DESCRIPTION: The Sawfish is really an elongated Ray, usually brown or rusty, whose snout extends to a long, hard beak or "saw," fitted with sharp teeth.

SIZE: Anglers are more apt to encounter small specimens, 2-6 feet long, but the Sawfish can reach monstrous sizes. World record 890 pounds, 8 ounces.

FOOD VALUE: Good.

GAME QUALITIES: Poor, unless very large.

TACKLE: Small ones are seldom targeted.

LURES AND BAITS: Whole dead Mullet or other fish.

RANGE: *Gulf of California, Mexico, to Panama. It's an oddity everywhere.*

HABITAT: *Likes mud or sand bottom of lagoons and estuaries, and will wander far up freshwater streams.*

Usually wearing brilliant colors and often packed into dense schools, Grunts are familiar to divers and reef fishermen throughout the tropics. Although not large enough to rate as great sport fish, they are fun to catch and make fine table fare. Moreover, they are usually willing to bite, even when more desirable bottom species play hard to get. Many anglers fish for Grunts not for food or fun but for bait. They generally make a superb offering for the large Groupers, Snappers and other predatory fish that share their reef habitat. Grunts belong to a large family. Although most of the members do reside on those aforementioned tropical reefs, some are more at home close to shore over grass or shell flats, and a couple of hardier species are found in California waters. The Sargo, in fact, was introduced to the Salton Sea, where it has done so well that it is now the No. 1 catch of fishermen in that salty inland lake— and also the No. 1 forage species for the Orangemouth Corvina, another happy introduction there (see Chapter 5).

The Grunts

Blackbar Grunt

Brassy Grunt

Burrito Grunt

Latin Grunt

Mojarra Grunt

Pacific Grunt

Pacific Porkfish

Salema

Sargo

Spottail Grunt

Wavyline Grunt

Blackbar Grunt

Anisotremus dovii

OTHER NAMES:

Spotted Head Sargo

RANGE: *Baja California, Mexico, to Panama.*

WHERE TO FISH: *Not strictly a reef dweller but found over hard bottom from near shore and in bays out to 50 feet or more.*

DESCRIPTION: The body is deep and the dorsal spines sharp. Color is dusky gray with four or five vertical black bars.

SIZE: A large Grunt, it frequently weighs more than a pound. Top weight is perhaps 3 pounds.

FOOD VALUE: Very good.

GAME QUALITIES: No softy on light tackle, it pulls hard and digs deep.

TACKLE: Spinning, baitcasting, light ocean gear.

LURES AND BAITS: Often hits small jigs fished for other species, but is more likely to fall for minnows, small cut baits, or shrimp.

Brassy Grunt

Orthopristis chalceus

RANGE: *Gulf of California, Mexico, to Peru.*

WHERE TO FISH: *Not a reef-dweller like most other Grunts, it ranges widely over both hard and soft bottoms, often very close to shore and seldom in more than about 20 feet of water.*

DESCRIPTION: Color is gray or silver with orange or brassy streaks. The pectoral fins are yellowish and other fins are dusky black.

SIZE: Most run about 7 or 8 inches, but it can reach 12 or more.

FOOD VALUE: Good.

GAME QUALITIES: Spunky on very light line.

TACKLE: Spinning gear.

LURES AND BAITS: Often hits small jigs fished for other species, but is more likely to fall for minnows, small cut baits, or shrimp.

Anisotremus interruptus

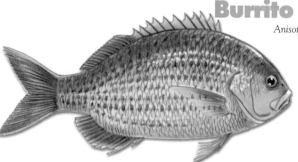

DESCRIPTION: Color is silvery overall, with gold sheen. Spots in center of each scale. Fins are brownish to yellow and the tail is yellow.

SIZE: Averages a pound or better and can top 5 pounds. World record 7 pounds, 14 ounces.

FOOD VALUE: Good.

GAME QUALITIES: Husky enough to give a tough fight on light line.

TACKLE: Spinning or baitcasting.

LURES AND BAITS: For quantity, use natural baits, especially shrimp or other shellfish. They can also be coaxed into taking small leadhead jigs.

RANGE: *Gulf of California, Mexico to Panama.*

WHERE TO FISH: *Reefs and rocks, especially where holes and caves are numerous. Also forages in surf and along rocky shores.*

Latin Grunt

Haemulon steindachneri

DESCRIPTION: Here's another Grunt with a black tail spot but its stripes are lighter than the Spottail.

SIZE: Averages around 8 inches but often exceeds a foot.

FOOD VALUE: Very good.

GAME QUALITIES: Not much.

TACKLE: Seldom targeted but easily taken on spinning.

LURES AND BAITS: Cut fish, shrimp or squid, fished on or near bottom.

RANGE: *Baja California, Mexico, to Panama.*

WHERE TO FISH: *They seem to cruise sandy areas around reefs, rather than the reefs themselves. Like other Grunts they forage a wide range of bottoms at night.*

Mojarra Grunt
Haemulon scudderii

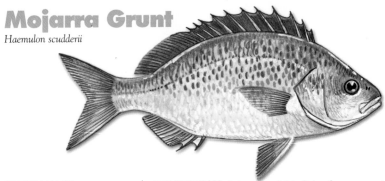

OTHER NAMES:

Grey Grunt

RANGE: *Baja California, Mexico, to Panama.*

WHERE TO FISH: *Over reefs in daytime and sandy or broken areas around reefs at night. They also are common around structure in many places.*

DESCRIPTION: Schools of this fish often are neighbors to schools of the Spottail Grunt but they are easy to distinguish. The scale spots are black and do not align into rows. Nor is there a black spot on the tail.

SIZE: Averages 8 or 10 inches; reaches 18 inches.

FOOD VALUE: Very good.

GAME QUALITIES: Not much.

TACKLE: Seldom targeted but easily caught on spinning gear.

LURES AND BAITS: Cut fish, shrimp or squid, fished on or near bottom.

Pacific Grunt
Anisotremus pacifici

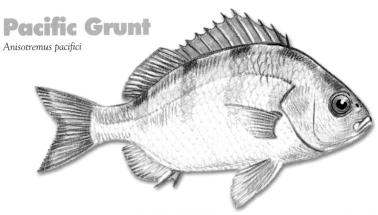

OTHER NAMES:

Carruco Sargo

RANGE: *Baja California, Mexico, to Panama.*

WHERE TO FISH: *Shallow coastal areas over hard or rocky bottom.*

DESCRIPTION: Color is silvery overall with vertical black bars that fade after death. Fins and tail are dusky.

SIZE: Up to a foot long.

FOOD VALUE: Good.

GAME QUALITIES: Spunky but limited by size.

TACKLE: Seldom targeted but easily taken on spinning.

LURES AND BAITS: Cut fish, shrimp or squid.

DESCRIPTION: This gaudy fellow is a familiar decoration on tropical reefs, although not as omnipresent as other Grunts. It is bright yellow or gold in background color.

SIZE: Averages a pound, sometimes hits 2 pounds.

FOOD VALUE: Good.

GAME QUALITIES: Fair for its size.

TACKLE: Seldom targeted but easily taken on spinning.

LURES AND BAITS: Cut fish, shrimp or squid.

OTHER NAMES:

Panama Porkfish

RANGE: *Baja California, Mexico, to Panama.*

WHERE TO FISH: *They stick close to rugged reef structure.*

Salema
Xenistius californiensis

DESCRIPTION: Color is shiny blue or green above and silvery below, with several yellow lengthwise stripes.

SIZE: Averages 6 inches; maximum 10 inches.

FOOD VALUE: A tasty panfish.

GAME QUALITIES: Poor because of size.

TACKLE: Seldom targeted except by youngsters.

LURES AND BAITS: Sometimes take a tiny jig, but respond much better to bits of shrimp or squid.

RANGE: *Central California to Panama.*

WHERE TO FISH: *Likes rocks, pilings and kelp beds from near shore out to about 30 feet.*

Sargo

Anisotremus davidsoni

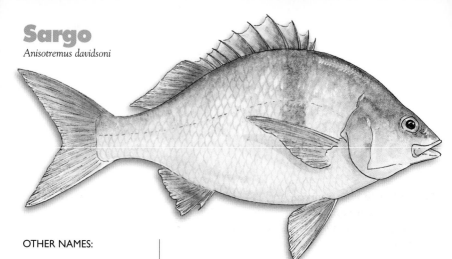

OTHER NAMES:

Sargo Grunt
China Croaker

RANGE: *Central California to the Gulf of California, Mexico.*

WHERE TO FISH: *Best spots are close to shore around kelp, grass and rocks. Many are taken from jetties and piers. Also found farther offshore.*

DESCRIPTION: Overall silver with a yellowish tinge and one prominent black bar extending downward on the side from under the dorsal fin to about the pectoral fin. Thick lips.

SIZE: Fish weighing 1-2 pounds are common; sometimes exceeds 3 pounds.

FOOD VALUE: Very good.

GAME QUALITIES: Tough fighter but a lightweight.

TACKLE: Pole, light spinning and baitcasting.

LURES AND BAITS: Lures seldom produce. Shrimp, crab and other shellfish are good bets.

Spottail Grunt

Haemulon maculicauda

DESCRIPTION: It is identifiable at a glance by white centers of its scales, which form a pattern of lengthwise stripes, and also, of course, by the namesake spot on its tail.

SIZE: Averages 6-8 inches; reaches a foot or so.

FOOD VALUE: A very tasty panfish.

GAME QUALITIES: Poor.

TACKLE: Pole or light spinning. Often targeted by anglers as bait for Groupers and other reef predators.

LURES AND BAITS: Any small piece of cut bait, whether from fish or shellfish.

RANGE: *Baja California, Mexico, to Panama.*

WHERE TO FISH: *Schools densely over reefs and patches but is also common inshore and can easily be caught from many docks and other shoreline spots.*

Wavyline Grunt

Microlepidotus inornatus

DESCRIPTION: Very similar in superficial appearance to the Salema, but the dorsal fin is continuous. No cause for confusion in California where the Salema is common, because the Wavyline Grunt seldom wanders that far north.

SIZE: Averages 6-8 inches; reaches a foot or more.

FOOD VALUE: Very good.

GAME QUALITIES: Spunky but limited by size.

TACKLE: Seldom targeted but easily caught on spinning gear.

LURES AND BAITS: Cut fish, shrimp or squid. Will also take small jigs.

RANGE: *Baja California, Mexico, and the Gulf of California.*

WHERE TO FISH: *Reef and rocky areas, especially at night.*

As a group, these fish comprise the minor leaguers of the Pacific sportfishing scene. Although some, such as the Porgy, Bobo, Whitefish, Opaleye and Triggerfish, are fine to eat and welcomed by many fishermen when bigger game is not at hand, most of the others are types that nearly all anglers would just as soon avoid, inasmuch as they are viewed as either bait-stealers or time-consumers, or perhaps even as threats to the angler's welfare. Included in the "menacing" category are Morays, Catfishes, Needlefishes, Cutlassfish and Puffers, all of which can painfully bite, scratch or stab if their captors do not take steps to avoid such injuries. Some Puffers, moreover, are unsafe to eat. Because this is a catch-all category, it also encompasses species that may be familiar to anglers in various Pacific waters, yet are seldom caught by them. Examples would be the Angelfishes and Parrotfishes, which are staples of tropical reefs, plus Mullets, Mojarras and a few others that inhabit coastal shallows.

A Miscellany

Pacific Porgy

Ocean Whitefish

Opaleye

Pacific Spadefish

California Moray

California Lizardfish

Bullseye Puffer

Mojarra

Azure Parrotfish

Finescale Triggerfish

Cutlassfish

King Angelfish

Chihuil

Long-Barbled Catfish

Pacific Needlefish

Barred Needlefish

Sharksucker

Remora

White Mullet

Striped Mullet

Hawaiian Bigeye

Yellow Bobo

Pacific Porgy

Calamus brachysomus

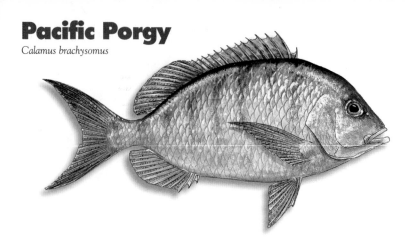

OTHER NAMES:

Pluma

RANGE: *Southern California to Panama, including Gulf of California, Mexico.*

WHERE TO FISH: *Found over a variety of bottom types and in depths from shore out to about 50 feet. They like grass but seem to prefer variegated bottom that mixes grass, sand and rock. They are popular targets from docks and piers in Mexico and Central America.*

DESCRIPTION: Silvery sides with dark blotches over sides, fins and tail, give this Porgy a camouflaged appearance that hides it well in grass. A vertical bar runs through the eye.

SIZE: Averages around 1 pound; sometimes hits 2 pounds.

FOOD VALUE: Very good.

GAME QUALITIES: Quite strong for its size; fast and stubborn fighter.

TACKLE: Light spinning and baitcasting tackle are best, although many different outfits are used with effect.

LURES AND BAITS: Although caught only occasionally on an artificial jig, Porgies are ready biters on shrimp, squid and various cut baits.

Ocean Whitefish

Caulolatilus princeps

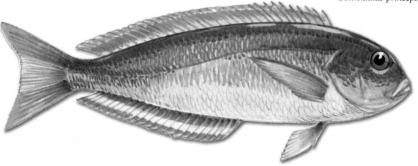

DESCRIPTION: The lower sides are white and dorsal surface and upper sides brownish or rusty. The dorsal fin is long and continuous, beginning above the pectoral and running nearly to the tail. The head is rounded and the fins are mostly edged in yellow, with streaks of blue-green.

SIZE: Averages 2-4 pounds; occasionally tops 10 pounds. World record 12 pounds, 11 ounces.

FOOD VALUE: Very good.

GAME QUALITIES: Nothing special; caught mostly on heavy gear.

TACKLE: Bottom-fishing outfits.

LURES AND BAITS: Whitefish are democratic feeders and will take many kinds of shellfish baits, small fish and cut baits.

OTHER NAMES:

Tilefish

RANGE: *Central California to Panama.*

WHERE TO FISH: *Near bottom around rocky areas in 30 to 250 feet of water, especially around the islands. They like sandy bottom near the rocks.*

Opaleye

Girella nigricans

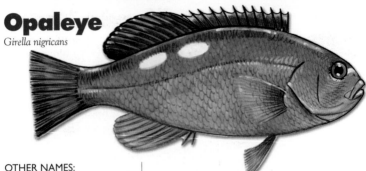

OTHER NAMES:

Sea Chub

RANGE: *San Francisco, California, to southern Baja California, Mexico. A similar species, inhabiting the Gulf of California, has three or four spots instead of the usual two.*

WHERE TO FISH: *Around rocks, rocky shorelines and jetties and around kelp beds, mostly near shore but sometimes to 100 feet.*

DESCRIPTION: Color is largely green or bluish-gray with two pale white spots on the upper sides and, usually, a white bar across the front of the head. The nose is rounded and the mouth is small.

SIZE: Most run 12-15 inches; maximum is about 2 feet.

FOOD VALUE: Good.

GAME QUALITIES: Wages a strong battle on light tackle.

TACKLE: Light gear provides much sport.

LURES AND BAITS: Although they feed primarily on seaweed, they will also take bits of cut shellfish, such as squid, shrimp or abalone scraps.

Pacific Spadefish

Chaetodipterus zonatus

OTHER NAMES:

Striped Angelfish

RANGE: *Southern California to Panama, including the Gulf of California, Mexico.*

WHERE TO FISH: *Likes a variety of structure, from shoreline piers and pilings to offshore reefs and rubble. Common around many navigation markers.*

DESCRIPTION: Superficially similar to the Angelfishes, the divided dorsal, and the color, are giveaways. The body is very deep and rounded. First rays of the posterior dorsal and anal fin are long and pointed.

SIZE: Averages 2-3 pounds; occasionally tops 10.

FOOD VALUE: Good.

GAME QUALITIES: Difficult to hook, but a strong, Jack-like fighter.

TACKLE: Any sort of light gear.

LURES AND BAITS: Spadefish feed on a variety of invertebrate animals and are usually caught on shrimp.

California Moray
Gymnothorax mordax

DESCRIPTION: Several species of Moray Eels inhabit the rocks and reefs of our covered area, most of them in tropical waters of Latin America and Hawaii. Most species are more colorful than this one but, because it is the common Moray of California and Baja, it is familiar to many more fishermen and divers than the others. The California Moray is solid green or brown.

SIZE: Averages 2-3 feet but can exceed 5 feet.

FOOD VALUE: Edible, but unappetizing to most.

GAME QUALITIES: Hooked Morays are tough to pull out of their holes, but the real fight comes after they are landed. It's best to cut the line.

TACKLE: Never targeted, but caught accidentally.

RANGE: *Southern California through Baja California, Mexico.*

WHERE TO FISH: *Both inshore and in deep water, wherever there are holes or crevices, such as around rocks, reefs, jetties, pilings or wrecks.*

California Lizardfish
Synodus lucioceps

DESCRIPTION: The coloration runs to shades of brown or reddish with dark blotches on the sides.

SIZE: Averages 10 or 12 inches, but some larger.

FOOD VALUE: Poor. The meat is white but very bony.

GAME QUALITIES: They are vicious and persistent strikers, but lack size or muscle to offer much resistance.

TACKLE: Anything goes. Not targeted, Lizardfish are strictly nuisances that horn in on efforts to catch more desirable fish.

LURES AND BAITS: They strike small live baits and any cut bait. They also attack bottom-bumping jigs with vigor—even lures as large as themselves.

OTHER NAMES:

Snakefish
Lagarto

RANGE: *From Northern California to Baja California, Mexico. Similar types extend to Panama.*

WHERE TO FISH: *They lurk over (or just under) sandy or soft bottom, anywhere from the shoreline out to 300 feet of water or more.*

Bullseye Puffer

Sphoeroides annulatus

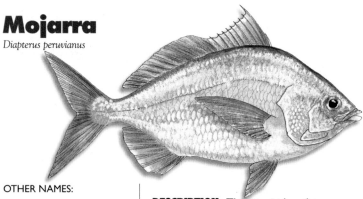

OTHER NAMES:

Blowfish
Swellfish

RANGE: *California to Panama.*

WHERE TO FISH: *At home in many shallow habitats. Usually prefers soft bottom and protected water but also found around jetties, where it is sheltered by the rocks.*

DESCRIPTION: This familiar species represents a group of very similar Puffers. It is identified by the target-like rings that show a "bull's eye" when viewed from above. Other species of inshore Puffers are colored somewhat the same.

SIZE: Most types average a foot or less.

FOOD VALUE: Excellent. Unfortunately, however, improper cleaning can lead to serious, even fatal, poisoning.

GAME QUALITIES: Not much sport on any size line.

TACKLE: Not often targeted.

LURES AND BAITS: As long-suffering inshore anglers know, Blowfish will hit many kinds of lures.

Mojarra

Diapterus peruvianus

OTHER NAMES:

Shad
Punchmouth
Silver Perch
Shiner

RANGE: *Baja California, Mexico, to Panama.*

WHERE TO FISH: *All types prefer shallow, calm water with mud or sand bottom, whether along the coast or well inside estuaries.*

DESCRIPTION: The tropical angler may encounter several kinds of Mojarras, all much alike in outline and color but varying somewhat in size. They are flashy silver in color, deep-bodied and with protractile mouths.

SIZE: From 3 or 4 inches to, occasionally, a pound or so.

FOOD VALUE: If large enough, they make fine panfish.

GAME QUALITIES: Willing but too small.

TACKLE: Light spinning gear or poles.

LURES AND BAITS: Tiny bits of shrimp, squid, cut fish.

Azure Parrotfish

Scarus compressus

DESCRIPTION: Parrotfishes come in many colors and this one was chosen because it comes in many colors itself.

SIZE: Adults of some species can top 3 feet in length.

FOOD VALUE: Not usually eaten.

GAME QUALITIES: Little tested, but strong.

TACKLE: Bottom-fishing gear.

LURES AND BAITS: None reliable.

OTHER NAMES:

Loro

Uhu

RANGE: *Various types are common from Baja California, Mexico, to Panama; also Hawaii.*

WHERE TO FISH: *Not targeted, a rare one is taken from the reefs.*

Finescale Triggerfish

Balistes polylepis

DESCRIPTION: Triggerfish species of our waters look much alike. Many have "triggers" whereby front dorsals lock solid but can be folded with a light touch on the small dorsal.

SIZE: Most catches run from 1 to 3 pounds.

FOOD VALUE: Excellent.

GAME QUALITIES: Tough to hook but very game.

TACKLE: If targeting Triggers specifically, light spinning or baitcasting gear is best. Hooks must be small.

LURES AND BAITS: Triggers bite any sort of cutbait.

OTHER NAMES:

Turbot

Tall

RANGE: *Baja California, Mexico, to Panama.*

WHERE TO FISH: *Reefs, rocky areas and dropoffs; occasionally inshore and in bays.*

Cutlassfish

Trichiurus lepturus

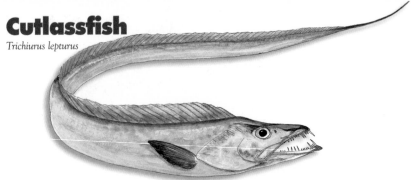

OTHER NAMES:

Ribbonfish
Threadtail

RANGE: *California to Panama.*

WHERE TO FISH: *Open coastal waters, plus bays, inlets and coastal streams. Often found in company with other schooling species.*

DESCRIPTION: A large and menacing mouth with numerous fang-like teeth give this lightweight a deceptively fearsome appearance, but the only danger to the angler lies in his own carelessness.

SIZE: Average is about 2 feet, with an occasional one running to 4 feet. World record 8 pounds, 1 ounce.

FOOD VALUE: Poor. There is little meat and it is quite bony.

GAME QUALITIES: A lightweight with little fight.

TACKLE: Seldom targeted; taken on light gear.

LURES AND BAITS: Live small baitfish best.

King Angelfish

Holacanthus passer

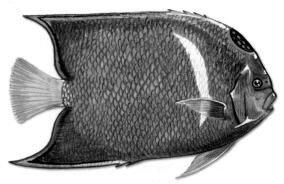

OTHER NAMES:

Cachama

RANGE: *Baja California, Mexico, to Panama (others in Hawaii).*

WHERE TO FISH: *Not targeted, they mostly cruise clear-water reefs.*

DESCRIPTION: Angels, like Parrotfishes, are graceful and usually brilliant fixtures of most tropical reefs. This one and the Cortez Angelfish (*H. zonipectus*) are the most familiar in our range.

SIZE: Most run 12-18 inches in length.

FOOD VALUE: Seldom eaten; reported to be good.

GAME QUALITIES: Not often tested.

TACKLE: Light spinning or baitcasting.

LURES AND BAITS: Tiny baits if any.

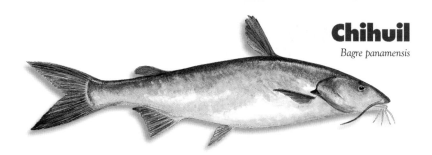

Chihuil
Bagre panamensis

DESCRIPTION: Several species of marine Catfish, of which this is probably the most common, occur in our range. To anglers they look much the same and all are cursed indiscriminately.

SIZE: Average weight is around 2 pounds.

FOOD VALUE: Good but usually shunned by anglers.

GAME QUALITIES: Not bad at first.

TACKLE: Only light gear can provide much sport.

LURES AND BAITS: You name it.

OTHER NAMES:

Catfish
Sea Catfish
Bagre del Mar

RANGE: *Southern California to Panama.*

WHERE TO FISH: *Muddy or soft bottoms, either offshore or in estuaries.*

Long-Barbled Catfish
Bagre pinnimaculatus

DESCRIPTION: While the color is much the same, this one differs from other or "common" Catfishes in having long streamers flowing from the first dorsal fin and the ventral fins. The streamers do not make these fish any more dangerous. It's the short spines just beneath them that are more dangerous.

SIZE: Larger than other Cats, to 6 pounds.

FOOD VALUE: More highly regarded as table fare than other marine Cats.

GAME QUALITIES: Surprisingly tough fight.

TACKLE: Any sort of casting gear is good (except fly).

LURES AND BAITS: Live bait and many lures.

OTHER NAMES:

Gafftopsail Catfish
Bandera

RANGE: *Gulf of California, Mexico, to Ecuador.*

WHERE TO FISH: *No telling where you might encounter them in coastal waters, estuaries and river mouths, but they do seem to prefer the edges of channels and holes.*

Pacific Needlefish

Tylosurus acus pacificus

OTHER NAMES:

Agujon

RANGE: *Southern Baja California, Mexico, to Panama.*

WHERE TO FISH: *Stays at the surface, both inshore and offshore; common along shorelines and also over reefs.*

DESCRIPTION: The shape is long and needle-like. The long bill is studded with many sharp teeth. Color is green above, white below. Dorsal and anal fins are situated jut forward of the tail.

SIZE: Averages 18 inches to 2 feet; sometimes grows to 4 feet.

FOOD VALUE: Quite good, but green flesh turns off many people.

GAME QUALITIES: Hardly any, but nuisance value is high.

TACKLE: Generally, you have no choice.

LURES AND BAITS: Needlefish democratically attack nearly any small lure or natural bait—usually to the angler's distress.

Barred Needlefish

Ablennes hians

OTHER NAMES:

Flat Needlefish
Agujon
Gar

RANGE: *Baja California, Mexico, to Panama.*

WHERE TO FISH: *Most are caught offshore but some enter estuaries; always at the surface.*

DESCRIPTION: Similar to the Pacific needlefish in color but has several dark bars on the side near the tail. The shape is also flatter.

SIZE: Averages 18 inches to 2 feet; sometimes grows to 4 feet.

FOOD VALUE: Good, and a good seller in Latin markets although the flesh is green.

GAME QUALITIES: Light weight lacks punch, but fight is acrobatic.

TACKLE: Only the lightest would provide sport.

LURES AND BAITS: Like the Pacific Needlefish, this fellow is ready to pounce on nearly any small lure or natural bait—usually to the angler's distress.

Sharksucker

Echeneis naucrates

DESCRIPTION: The head is flat and fitted with a sucking disc. Overall color is dark with a vivid white strip running lengthwise. This is the most familiar of several closely related "hitchhiking" fishes.

SIZE: Usually 1 foot or less, but can exceed 3 feet. World record 5 pounds, 1 ounce.

FOOD VALUE: Poor.

GAME QUALITIES: Not a bad fighter for its size.

TACKLE: Never targeted, but often caught on all sorts of gear.

LURES AND BAITS: Any kind of natural bait or small lure.

OTHER NAMES:

Remora

RANGE: *Southern California to Panama; also Hawaii.*

WHERE TO FISH: *Mostly offshore but also come into coastal waters.*

Remora

Remora remora

DESCRIPTION: This is another sucking species that is solid in color—usually gray or charcoal—and lacks the stripe of the preceding type. It also has a rounder head.

SIZE: From a few inches to a couple of feet. World record 2 pounds, 6 ounces.

FOOD VALUE: Nil.

GAME QUALITIES: Not much fight.

TACKLE: Never targeted and caught less often than the preceding species.

LURES AND BAITS: The Remora will take nearly any kind of natural bait or small lure it can swallow.

OTHER NAMES:

Sharksucker

RANGE: *Southern California to Panama; also Hawaii.*

WHERE TO FISH: *Free-roaming, usually offshore. Attaches mainly to Sharks.*

White Mullet

Mugil curema

OTHER NAMES:

Silver Mullet
Lisa Blanca
Liseta

RANGE: *Baja California, Mexico, to Panama.*

WHERE TO FISH: *Shallow coastal waters. Roams into fresh water.*

DESCRIPTION: Generally smaller than Black Mullet and lighter in color. The stripes are also less noticeable, or absent. The tail is not so deeply forked, but the most obvious distinguishing feature is the tail is edged in black.

SIZE: Averages a pound but can exceed 3 pounds. World record 1 pound, 7 ounces.

FOOD VALUE: Good.

GAME QUALITIES: A spirited fighter for its size.

TACKLE: Poles or light spinning and baitcasting gear.

LURES AND BAITS: Same baits as for Black Mullet.

Striped Mullet

Mugil cephalus

OTHER NAMES:

Black Mullet
Lisa
'ama 'ama

RANGE: *Southern California to Panama; also Hawaii.*

WHERE TO FISH: *Shallow coastal waters and bays; ventures far into fresh water.*

DESCRIPTION: The head is round and the mouth tiny. Back and upper sides are dark gray; lower sides and belly are silvery. Several longitudinal stripes generally apparent. Tail is deeply forked and solid in color.

SIZE: Most run from 1-3 pounds, but 5-pounders are often seen. World record 6 pounds, 15 ounces.

FOOD VALUE: Excellent, but depends on personal taste.

GAME QUALITIES: A wild, surface-cutting fighter.

TACKLE: Fishing for mullet requires more patience than most anglers possess. Cast-netting is the best approach.

LURES AND BAITS: Mullet primarily feed on algae but will sometimes take a bait into their mouth.

Hawaiian Bigeye

Priacanthus alalaua

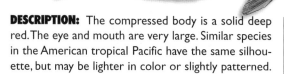

DESCRIPTION: The compressed body is a solid deep red. The eye and mouth are very large. Similar species in the American tropical Pacific have the same silhouette, but may be lighter in color or slightly patterned.

SIZE: Less than a foot.

FOOD VALUE: Pretty good; not much meat.

GAME QUALITIES: Minor.

TACKLE: All sorts of bottom-fishing tackle.

LURES AND BAITS: Pieces of fish or shellfish.

OTHER NAMES:

Toro

aweoweo

RANGE: *Hawaii. This and similar ones also occur from Baja California, Mexico, to Panama.*

WHERE TO FISH: *Coral reefs and rocky areas, usually from 30 feet or so to very deep ledges, at least 600 feet.*

Yellow Bobo

Polydactylus opercularis

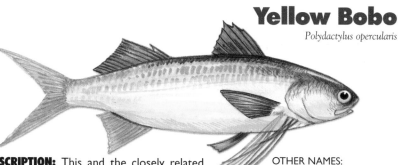

DESCRIPTION: This and the closely related Blue Bobo (*P. approximans*) are often found in the same waters. The Yellow species has an overall yellowish or brownish cast, while the Blue type is blue-gray in color. Both have the typical "threads" at the base of the pectoral fins. Their heads are blunt or rounded, with underslung lower jaws.

SIZE: Both average 12-16 inches.

FOOD VALUE: Good.

GAME QUALITIES: A lightweight; not much fight.

TACKLE: Very light spinning or casting gear.

LURES AND BAITS: They feed mostly on crustaceans and so the best baits are shrimp, crabs and marine worms.

OTHER NAMES:

Yellow Threadfin

RANGE: *Southern California to Panama.*

WHERE TO FISH: *Bobos are often found in the tumbling surf, but they frequent quieter waters as well, both along the coast and in bays and harbors.*

Many of the fish in this chapter cause mixed emotions on the part of anglers: To eat or to use for bait? Herrings and Smelts are among the most popular and productive of baitfishes, but at the same time, several species of them are highly regarded as food, and at least one, the American Shad, is a light-tackle game fish of the highest order. Just what makes a baitfish anyway? Nearly every fish in the sea, much to its distress, could lay legitimate claim to that status at one stage or another of its life cycle. Anglers, however, generally think of baitfish as any of a wide variety of silvery, schooling species whose main purpose in life seems to be filling the bellies of predatory gamesters and the baitwells of sportfishing boats. Herrings are highly prominent in that thinking, as are Smelts, Candlefish and Anchovies. Sardines, which also are high-ranking members of the baitfish group, are actually a type of Herring. Of course, numerous species of entirely different families are also bait staples, including Mullet, Halfbeaks and certain small Jacks and Mackerels. In addition, most experienced anglers have long since come to realize that when the baitfish of choice is not available, many substitute species of appropriate size are quite likely to produce the desired results.

Herrings and Baitfishes

American Shad

California Grunion

California Killifish

Capelin

Deepbody Anchovy

Eulachon

Jacksmelt

Longfin Halfbeak

Longfin Smelt

Northern Anchovy

Pacific Herring

Pacific Sand Lance

Pacific Sardine

Pacific Saury

Rainbow Smelt

Round Herring

Surf Smelt

Thread Herring

Threadfin Shad

Whitebait Smelt

American Shad

Alosa sapidissima

OTHER NAMES:

Common Shad

RANGE: *Alaska to southern California.*

WHERE TO FISH: *Many rivers enjoy runs of Shad, which live at sea but return to spawn in spring. Although much of the angling activity takes place in fresh water, many are taken in estuaries and river mouths.*

DESCRIPTION: Enjoys a following as avid as that of the Striped Bass. Its color is blue to dark green above with silvery sides and a sharp ridge on the belly. A dark spot just aft of the gill cover near the back is followed by a series of smaller black dots.

SIZE: Most run 1-4 pounds, with 6-pounders taken on occasion. World record 11 pounds, 4 ounces.

FOOD VALUE: Fillets excellent, if bony. Roe a delicacy.

GAME QUALITIES: Nicknamed "freshwater Tarpon."

TACKLE: Caught with spinning or fly.

LURES AND BAITS: Since most strikes occur near bottom, the flyrod fancier must use a sinking line, or weighted flies, or both. A variety of small, flashy fly patterns will do the job, although most anglers, of course, have their own pets.

California Grunion

Leuresthes tenuis

OTHER NAMES:

Grunon

RANGE: *Central California to southern Baja California, Mexico.*

WHERE TO FISH: *Most famous "fishing" for Grunion takes place on southern California beaches at night during spring high tides when they spawn.*

DESCRIPTION: Very slender with frontal protruding mouth. Color is green above with silver side stripes.

SIZE: Most are well under 6 inches, but some may reach around 7 inches.

FOOD VALUE: Very good.

GAME QUALITIES: None.

TACKLE: Bare hands are the only legal "tackle" on the beaches.

LURES AND BAITS: Not targeted with hook and line.

California Killifish

Fundulus parvipinnis

DESCRIPTION: Green above and yellow below with several vertical bands. The single dorsal fin is centrally located. The tail is round.

SIZE: Most are only a couple of inches long; maximum is around 4 inches.

FOOD VALUE: None.

GAME QUALITIES: None, but kids catch them for fun and adults for bait.

TACKLE: Pole or lightest spinning outfit; also seines and minnow traps.

LURES AND BAITS: Tiny bits of cut fish, shrimp or squid.

OTHER NAMES:

Pacific Kilifish

RANGE: *Central California to northern Baja California, Mexico.*

WHERE TO FISH: *Tidal areas and salt marshes, close to shore and around grass or rough bottom.*

Capelin

Mallotus villosus

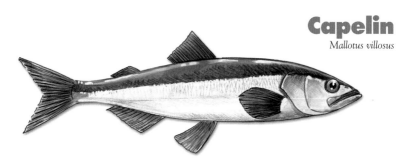

DESCRIPTION: Slender body. Color is olive green on top and silvery on the sides and belly.

SIZE: Averages 4-6 inches; reaches perhaps 8 inches.

FOOD VALUE: Very good.

GAME QUALITIES: None.

TACKLE: Nets.

LURES AND BAITS: Not a hook-and-line target.

RANGE: *Alaska and British Columbia.*

WHERE TO FISH: *An important forage and bait species, it spawns along gravel and sand beaches in warm months; schools offshore at other times.*

Deepbody Anchovy

Anchoa compressa

OTHER NAMES:

Anchoa

RANGE: *Central California to central Baja California, Mexico.*

WHERE TO FISH: *Most commonly taken in bays but found along the outer coast as well.*

DESCRIPTION: The deep, compressed body is a good identifier. The back is green and the underside white. There is a silver stripe on the sides. The mouth is large and underslung.

SIZE: Most run 3-4 inches; maximum is about 6 inches.

FOOD VALUE: Good but generally used as bait and chum.

GAME QUALITIES: None.

TACKLE: Nets.

LURES AND BAITS: Not a hook-and-line target.

Eulachon

Thaleichthys pacificus

OTHER NAMES:

Candlefish

RANGE: *Alaska to northern California.*

WHERE TO FISH: *Most are netted but many are caught by hand on beaches or tidal flats, where they burrow in the sand to spawn.*

DESCRIPTION: Color is brown or blue above, silver below. Tiny black dots on back.

SIZE: Averages 6-8 inches but can reach 10 inches.

FOOD VALUE: Good, but used far more often for bait; probably the No. 1 bait for Salmon.

GAME QUALITIES: None.

TACKLE: Nets, hands, rakes.

LURES AND BAITS: Not a hook-and-line target.

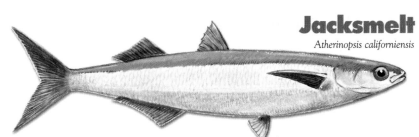

Jacksmelt
Atherinopsis californiensis

DESCRIPTION: Body is green above and white below with a silver stripe on the side. Small frontal mouth. A closely similar species, the Topsmelt, *A. affinis*, is slightly smaller. Anglers seldom bother to differentiate between them.

SIZE: Averages 12 inches of slightly more; may reach 18 inches.

FOOD VALUE: Good but more often sought as bait.

GAME QUALITIES: Not strong but spirited on light line.

TACKLE: Light spinning is best.

LURES AND BAITS: Small bits of cut fish, shrimp or squid. Will also take shiny, unbaited bait hooks at times.

RANGE: *Oregon to southern Baja California, Mexico.*

WHERE TO FISH: *Seems to prefer turbid water, usually close to shore. Many are caught from piers.*

Longfin Halfbeak
Hemiramphus saltator

DESCRIPTION: In the numerous types of Halfbeak, only the lower jaw is elongated, as opposed to the Needlefishes, in which both jaws are long and toothy, and the great Billfishes with their elongated upper jaws or "bills." This is the largest of the Pacific Halfbeaks and is a virtual dead ringer for the Atlantic Ballyhoo, being green to brown above and silver on the sides and belly. It is widely used as both a rigged trolling bait and as live or cut bait.

SIZE: Most run 10-12 inches; some reach 18 inches or more.

FOOD VALUE: Fair but seldom eaten by sportsmen.

GAME QUALITIES: Spunky and aerial-minded but without strength.

TACKLE: Most are caught with nets but they can be taken by chumming and fishing with tiny hooks.

LURES AND BAITS: Small bits of cut bait, floated in the chum without a sinker.

OTHER NAMES:

Pajarito
Ballyhoo

RANGE: *Southern California to Panama.*

WHERE TO FISH: *They school at the surface around rocks and reefs, or offshore around floating weeds and rips.*

Longfin Smelt

Spirinchus thaleichthys

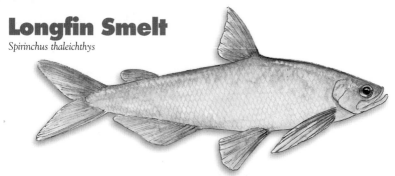

RANGE: *Alaska to central California.*

WHERE TO FISH: *Close to shore; also in coastal rivers.*

DESCRIPTION: Color is greenish brown above and silvery below, with no side stripe. The mouth is very large. Pectoral fin is longer than on other Smelts, reaching to or past the front of the pelvic fin.

SIZE: Generally less than 6 inches.

FOOD VALUE: Poor but good bait.

GAME QUALITIES: None.

TACKLE: Nets.

LURES AND BAITS: Not a hook-and-line target.

Northern Anchovy

Engraulis mordax

OTHER NAMES:

Pacific Anchovy
California
Anchovy
Anchoa

RANGE: *Vancouver Island, British Columbia, to Cabo San Lucas, Baja California, Mexico.*

WHERE TO FISH: *Usually the outside coast, from near shore out to 500 feet of water or more, but they also swarm harbors and bays at times.*

DESCRIPTION: The body is round, not compressed. The back is blue or greenish and the underside white. The mouth is underslung. The nose is pointed and so is the gill cover.

SIZE: Averages 3-5 inches, but many run 6-7 inches.

FOOD VALUE: Pretty good, but sought mostly as bait.

GAME QUALITIES: Fun but no challenge.

TACKLE: Nets; snatch hooks; poles or light spinning gear.

LURES AND BAITS: On lines, most are snagged but they will take tiny, bright hooks, either singly or on multi-hook bait-catching rigs.

Pacific Herring

Clupea pallasii

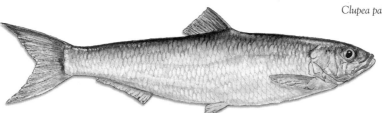

DESCRIPTION: Dark blue to olive above, shading to silver below. No dark spots on body or fins.

SIZE: Averages 6-8 inches but is not rare at 10-12 inches.

FOOD VALUE: Debatable. Very good pickled or smoked.

GAME QUALITIES: Tough little battler on suitable tackle.

TACKLE: Most fishing is for bait with light spinning tackle.

LURES AND BAITS: Small minnows or shrimp top the list of natural baits. Tiny spoons and jigs are very productive, as are multi-hook bait-catching rigs.

OTHER NAMES:

Herring
Sardina

RANGE: Alaska to northern Baja California, Mexico.

WHERE TO FISH: Close inshore and in estuaries during breeding periods of spring and early summer. Usually found in fairly large schools, though not so dense as in the past.

Pacific Sand Lance

Ammodytes hexapterus

DESCRIPTION: Slender and round-bodied with a pointed snout, the Sand Lance resembles a small Eel, but an obvious point of distinction is the forked tail, which is separate from the dorsal and anal fins. Color is brownish above, silvery below, often with a blue stripe on the side.

SIZE: Up to about 6 inches.

FOOD VALUE: Good but used mostly as bait.

GAME QUALITIES: None.

TACKLE: Nets, rakes, bare hands.

BAITS AND LURES: Not a hook-and-line target.

OTHER NAMES:

Sand Eel
Lancefish

RANGE: Alaska to southern California.

WHERE TO FISH: It hides by burrowing several inches deep in soft sand of beaches, but also schools thickly both offshore and near shore.

Pacific Sardine

Sardinops sagax

OTHER NAMES:

California Sardine
Pilchard
Sardina

RANGE: *Alaska to northern Gulf of California, Mexico.*

WHERE TO FISH: *Large schools roam the coast, usually fairly near shore.*

DESCRIPTION: Color is dark green or blue above and silvery below. Body is elongated and thin. Scattered spots on upper side.

SIZE: Averages 6-8 inches but is common at 10-12 inches and may reach 16.

FOOD VALUE: Pretty good but not popular. Anglers like them mostly for bait.

GAME QUALITIES: Poor.

TACKLE: Nets. Light spinning.

LURES AND BAITS: Although they are plankton feeders they will sometimes go for shiny hooks on multi-hook bait-catching rigs or a single tiny jig or spoon.

Pacific Saury

Cololabis saira

RANGE: *Alaska to Mexico.*

WHERE TO FISH: *Offshore, near rips or floating weeds.*

DESCRIPTION: Dark green to blue on dorsal surface, silvery below, with small bright blue blotches scattered on the sides. Body is very slender and elongated.

SIZE: Averages 10 or 12 inches; reaches 14 or 15.

FOOD VALUE: Fair but anglers seek them mostly as bait, particularly for Tuna.

GAME QUALITIES: None.

TACKLE: Dipnets (lights attract them at night). They can also be caught in lesser number on tiny bait hooks.

LURES AND BAITS: Small strips of cut fish or squid.

Rainbow Smelt
Osmerus mordax

DESCRIPTION: Green or brown above, silvery below, often with a streak of darker silver down the side from gill to tail. Name comes from its iridescence. The teeth are small and pointed.

SIZE: Averages 6 or 8 inches; sometimes to 12 inches.

FOOD VALUE: Excellent fresh, if kept well iced. Also good when pickled or smoked. Also, of course, a fine baitfish.

GAME QUALITIES: Too small to be a challenge, but cooperative and fun.

TACKLE: Can be caught from beaches with hands or small nets; also with lightest rods or poles.

LURES AND BAITS: Tiny hooks baited with bits of shrimp, squid or marine worm.

OTHER NAMES:

Arctic Smelt
American Smelt
Pygmy Smelt

RANGE: *Alaska to southern California.*

WHERE TO FISH: *Not nearly so common as other Smelts, it stays close to shore and enters rivers to spawn. Most recreational catches are made in bays and river mouths.*

Round Herring
Etrumeus teres

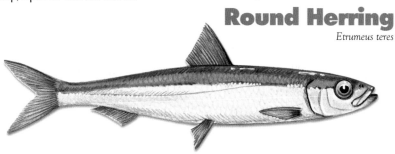

DESCRIPTION: Silver with an olive-green back. Cylindrical body. Belly is round and smooth, unlike other Herrings, which have keeled bellies.

SIZE: Averages 3 inches; grows to 10 or 12 inches.

FOOD VALUE: Very good, but better as bait.

GAME QUALITIES: None.

TACKLE: Nets. Seldom takes a hook.

LURES AND BAITS: None dependable.

OTHER NAMES:

Atlantic Round
Herring
California Round
Herring
Japanese Herring

RANGE: *Central California to Panama.*

WHERE TO FISH: *Large schools are mainly found inshore of 100 feet, but wander widely in deeper water too.*

Herrings and Baitfishes **261**

Surf Smelt

Hypomesus pretiosus

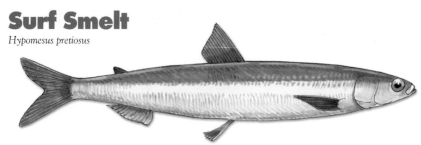

OTHER NAMES:

Silver Smelt
Day Fish
Day Smelt

RANGE: Alaska to southern California.

WHERE TO FISH: Generally caught during the day on beaches when they spawn. The Night Smelt spawns at night, frequently on the same beaches.

DESCRIPTION: Color is bluish above, silvery on side, with a silver stripe. The mouth is small. The superficially similar Night Smelt, *Spirinchus sparksi*, often found in the same waters, has a large mouth and teeth on the tongue.

SIZE: Averages 6-8 inches; not rare to 10 inches.

FOOD VALUE: Very good when dressed and fried whole.

GAME QUALITIES: Fun but no fight.

TACKLE: Caught on beach by hand or with nets. Also can be taken with pole or light spinning rod.

LURES AND BAITS: Multi-hook bait-catching rigs.

Thread Herring

Opisthonema libertate

OTHER NAMES:

Sardina machete

RANGE: Baja California, Mexico, including the Gulf of California, to Panama. Straggles to southern California.

WHERE TO FISH: Roams in large schools, usually near shore.

DESCRIPTION: Body is flat and the last ray of dorsal is long. Light blue above and silver below with tiny spots on the back. The similar Threadfin Shad has pointed nose and no spots. A related species, *O. medirastre*, is not so deep-bodied.

SIZE: Usually 8-10 inches.

FOOD VALUE: Poor, but it's a great and popular Tuna bait.

GAME QUALITIES: None.

TACKLE: Nets. Spinning tackle.

LURES AND BAITS: Sometimes falls for bait-catching rigs.

Threadfin Shad

Dorosoma petenense

DESCRIPTION: The back is blue to green and the sides silvery. Long "thread" extends from rear of dorsal fin. The snout is pointed and the mouth frontal. Black specks on inside and outside of lower jaw.

SIZE: Seldom more than 6 inches.

FOOD VALUE: None, but is an excellent bait.

GAME QUALITIES: None.

TACKLE: Nets. Seldom caught on a hook.

LURES AND BAITS: None dependable.

RANGE: *This is a common freshwater forage species that was introduced to California some 50 years ago and now is often encountered in tidewaters and bays, and even offshore to some extent in California and Oregon.*

WHERE TO FISH: *Schools in open water. In tidal rivers it prefers bends and eddies.*

Whitebait Smelt

Allosmerus elongatus

DESCRIPTION: Cylindrical body is a very pale green with a silver stripe. Single canine tooth in upper jaw.

SIZE: Averages 3-5 inches, but many run 6-7 inches.

FOOD VALUE: Not bad, but mostly utilized as bait.

GAME QUALITIES: Poor.

TACKLE: Nets. Can occasionally be taken on light line and tiny hooks.

LURES AND BAITS: Multi-hook bait rigs.

OTHER NAMES:

Whitebait

RANGE: *Vancouver Island, British Columbia, to central California.*

WHERE TO FISH: *Runs in thick schools, usually in bays.*

INDEX

African Pompano 40
Agujon 248
Ahi 29
Albacore 16
Allison Tuna 29
Almaco Jack 41
Amarillo Snapper 186
American Shad 254
American Smelt 261
Anchovy, Deepbody 256
Anchovy, Northern 258
Angel Shark 202
Angelfish, King 246
Arctic Char 110
Arctic Smelt 261
Atlantic Round Herring 261
Azure Parrotfish 245
Bairdiella 76
Banded Rockfish 143
Barracuda, Great 66
Barracuda, Pacific 68
Barred Needlefish 248
Barred Pargo 187
Barred Sand Bass 166
Barred Surfperch 120
Bass, Barred Sand 166
Bass, Black Sea 167
Bass, Giant Sea 167
Bass, Goldspotted Sand 171
Bass, Kelp 175
Bass, Spotted Sand 181
Bass, Striped 183
Bay Shark 208
Big Skate 226
Bigeye Jack 42
Bigeye Pollack 151
Bigeye Scad 43
Bigeye Snook 198
Bigeye Trevally 42
Bigeye Tuna 17
Bigeye, Hawaiian 251
Bigmouth Sole 96
Black Croaker 77
Black Jack 44
Black Marlin 32
Black Mullet 250
Black Perch 121
Black Rockfish 133
Black Sea Bass 133
Black Sea Bass 167
Black Skipjack 18
Black Snook 196
Black Surfperch 121
Black-and-Yellow Rockfish 132
Blackbar Grunt 232
Blackfin Snook 198
Blackspotted Trout 114
Blacktip Shark 203
Blowfish 244
Blue Cod 160
Blue Corvina 85

Blue Jack 45
Blue Marlin 33
Blue Rockfish 134
Blue Shark 204
Blue-and-Gold Snapper 188
Blueback 113
Blueback Char 110
Bluefin Jack 45
Bluefin Trevally 45
Bobo, Yellow 251
Bocaccio 134
Bonefish, Pacific 69
Bonito Shark 217
Bonito, Pacific 22
Bonito, Striped 27
Bonnethead 205
Brassy Grunt 232
Broadfin Flounder 105
Broomtail Grouper 168
Brown Jack 44
Brown Rockfish 135
Brown Shark 211
Bull Cod 160
Bull Shark 206
Bullet Mackerel 19
Bullseye Puffer 244
Burrito Grunt 233
Butter Sole 99
Butterlips 121
Cabezone 160
Cabrilla, Flag 169
Cabrilla, Spotted 180
Calico Grouper 175
Calico Salmon 112
Calico Surfperch 122
California Anchovy 258
California Bonito 22
California Corbina 78
California Grunion 254
California Halibut 97
California Horse Mackerel 49
California Killifish 255
California Lizardfish 243
California Moray 243
California Round Herring 261
California Sardine 260
California Scorpionfish 135
California Sheepshead 64
California Skate 227
California Whiting 78
Canary Rockfish 136
Candlefish 256
Capelin 255
Catalina Croaker 93
Catfish 247
Catfish, Long-Barbled 247
Char, Arctic 110
Chihuil 247
Chilepepper 136
China Croaker 77
China Rockfish 137

Chinook Salmon. 111
Chub, Sea 242
Chum Salmon. 112
C-O Sole 100
Cod, Blue 160
Cod, Bull. 160
Cod, Chili 136
Cod, China 137
Cod, Cutlass. 155
Cod, Pacific. 148
Cod, Rock. 135
Cod, Tiger. 143
Coho Salmon 113
Colorado Snapper 189
Common Greenling 157
Common Shad 254
Common Thresher. 207
Coney, Gulf. 173
Copper Rockfish 137
Corbina, California. 78
Corbina, Highfin 80
Corvina, Gulf 79
Corvina, Orangemouth 81
Corvina, Shortfin 85
Corvina, Stolzmann's 87
Corvina, Striped 88
Corvina, White 90
Cowcod 138
Croaker, Black 77
Croaker, China 77
Croaker, Romeo. 76
Croaker, Spotfin 86
Croaker, White. 91
Croaker, Yellowfin 93
Cutlass Cod 155
Cutlassfish. 246
Cutthroat Trout 114
Day Smelt. 262
Deepbody Anchovy 256
Diamond Turbot. 101
Dog Salmon 112
Dog Snapper, Pacific. 191
Dogfish, Blue. 204
Dolly Varden. 115
Dolphin. 65
Dorado. 65
Drum, Pacific 82
Drum, Yellowfin. 93
Dusky Shark 208
Eulachon. 256
Fall Salmon 112
Fantail Rockfish. 136
Finescale Triggerfish 245
Flag Cabrilla 169
Flag Grouper 169
Flat Needlefish 248
Flathead Sole 102
Flounder, Broadfin 105
Flounder, California 97
Flounder, Fringe 106
Flounder, Roundnose 104

Flounder, Scalyfin 99
Flounder, Starry 107
Freshwater Shark. 206
Frigate Mackerel 20
Fringe Flounder 106
Gafftopsail Catfish 247
Gafftopsail Pompano 46
Galapagos Shark. 209
Giant Halibut 103
Giant Hammerhead Shark 210
Giant Hawkfish. 170
Giant Sea Bass 167
Giant Trevally 60
Goggle-eye 43
Golden Croaker. 86
Golden Grouper 176
Golden Jack 47
Golden Trevally. 47
Goldspotted Sand Bass 171
Goliath Grouper 172
Grass Rockfish 138
Gray Cod 148
Gray Smoothhound 209
Grayfish. 220
Graysby, Panama. 177
Great Barracuda 66
Great Hammerhead. 210
Great White Shark. 222
Green Jack 48
Green Runner 48
Green Sturgeon 67
Greenling, Kelp. 154
Greenling, Rock 156
Greenling, Whitespotted 157
Greenspotted Rockfish 139
Ground Shark. 208
Grouper, Broomtail 168
Grouper, Calico 175
Grouper, Flag 169
Grouper, Golden 176
Grouper, Goliath 172
Grouper, Gulf 174
Grouper, Harlequin 170
Grouper, Leopard. 176
Grouper, Sawtail 178
Grouper, Snowy 179
Grouper, Spotted 180
Grouper, Starry 169
Grouper, Starstudded. 182
Grouper, Tiger 177
Grunion, California. 254
Grunt, Blackbar 232
Grunt, Brassy 232
Grunt, Burrito 233
Grunt, Latin 233
Grunt, Mojarra 234
Grunt, Pacific 234
Grunt, Sargo 236
Grunt, Spottail 237
Grunt, Wavyline 237
Guitarfish, Shovelnose 228

Gulf Coney 173
Gulf Corvina 79
Gulf Grouper 174
Gulf Mackerel 21
Gulf Sierra 21
Gulf Weakfish 79
Hake, Pacific 149
Halfbeak, Longfin 257
Halibut, California 97
Halibut, Pacific 103
Harlequin Grouper 170
Hawaiian Bigeye 251
Hawkfish, Giant 170
Herring, Pacific 259
Herring, Round 261
Herring, Thread 262
Highfin Kingcroaker 80
Horse-eye Jack 42
Humpback Salmon 116
Humpback Snook 199
Island Shark 209
Jack Mackerel 49
Jack, Almaco 41
Jack, Bigeye 42
Jack, Black 44
Jack, Blue 45
Jack, Golden 47
Jack, Green 48
Jack, Pacific Crevalle 52
Jack, Threadfin 59
Jacksmelt 257
Japanese Herring 261
Jewfish 172
Jordan's Snapper 190
Jorobado 53
Jurel 52
Kahala 61
Kelp Bass 175
Kelp Greenling 154
Kelp Rockfish 139
Killifish, California 255
King Angelfish 246
King Salmon 111
Kingcroaker, Highfin 80
Kingcroaker, Pacific 83
Ladyfish, Pacific 70
Lagarto 243
Lance, Pacific Sand 259
Largetooth Sawfish 229
Latin Grunt 233
Leatherjack 50
Lemon Shark 211
Leopard Grouper 176
Leopard Shark 212
Lingcod 155
Lisa Blanca 250
Little Snook 197
Lizardfish, California 243
Long-Barbled Catfish 247
Longfin Halfbeak 257
Longfin Pompano 55
Longfin Smelt 258
Longspine Snook 197
Lookdown, Pacific 53
Lord, Red Irish 162
Lord, Yellow Irish 163
Mackerel Shark 215
Mackerel Tuna 18
Mackerel, Bullet 19
Mackerel, Frigate 20
Mackerel, Gulf 21
Mackerel, Pacific 23
Mackerel, Sierra 24
Mackerel, Tinker 23
Mahi Mahi 65
Marlin, Black 32
Marlin, Blue 33
Marlin, Striped 36
Medium Red Salmon 113
Mexican Bonito 27
Mexican Scad 51
Mojarra 244
Mojarra Grunt 234
Moray, California 243
Mountain Trout 114
Mullet Snapper 190
Mullet, Black 250
Mullet, Silver 250
Mullet, Striped 250
Mullet, White 250
Needlefish, Barred 248
Needlefish, Pacific 248
Northern Anchovy 258
Northern Halibut 103
Nurse Shark 213
Ocean Whitefish 241
Oceanic Bonito 25
Oceanic Whitetip Shark 214
Olive Rockfish 140
Ono 28
Opaleye 242
Orange Rockfish 136
Orangemouth Corvina 81
Orangespotted Rockfish 140
Oriental Bonito 27
Pacific Amberjack 41, 61
Pacific Anchovy 258
Pacific Angel Shark 202
Pacific Barracuda 68
Pacific Blue Marlin 33
Pacific Bluefin Tuna 26
Pacific Bonefish 69
Pacific Bonito 22
Pacific Cod 148
Pacific Crevalle Jack 52
Pacific Cubera Snapper 191
Pacific Drum 82
Pacific Electric Ray 228
Pacific Graysby 177
Pacific Grunt 234
Pacific Hake 149
Pacific Halibut 103

Pacific Herring 259
Pacific Killifish. 255
Pacific Kingcroaker. 83
Pacific Ladyfish 70
Pacific Lookdown 53
Pacific Mackerel 23
Pacific Needlefish 248
Pacific Permit 54
Pacific Pollack 151
Pacific Pompano 55
Pacific Porgy 240
Pacific Porkfish 235
Pacific Red Snapper 192
Pacific Sailfish 34
Pacific Sand Lance. 259
Pacific Sanddab 98
Pacific Sardine. 260
Pacific Saury 260
Pacific Sharpnose Shark 215
Pacific Spadefish 242
Pacific Spanish Mackerel. 24
Pacific Staghorn Sculpin 161
Pacific Tomcod 150
Pacific Yellowtail 61
Paloma 46
Paloma Pompano 55
Palometa. 46
Panama Graysby 177
Panama Porkfish 235
Papagallo. 58
Pargo Colorado 189
Pargo Lisa 190
Pargo Rayado 188
Pargo, Barred 187
Parrotfish, Azure. 245
Perch, Black. 121
Perch, Shiner. 126
Perch, Silver 244
Permit, Pacific 54
Petrale Sole. 104
Pike Shark. 220
Pilotfish 56
Pink Salmon 116
Pinkfish 124
Pluma 240
Pollock, Walleye 151
Pompano, African 40
Pompano, Gafftopsail 46
Pompano, Paloma 55
Popeyed Turbot 100
Porgy, Pacific. 240
Porkfish, Pacific. 235
Puffer, Bullseye 244
Pygmy Smelt 261
Queenfish 84
Quillback Rockfish 140
Rainbow 117
Rainbow Runner. 57
Rainbow Smelt 261
Rainbow Surfperch. 123
Rapshead Rockfish 145

Ray, Pacific Electric 228
Ray, Torpedo 228
Red Greenling 156
Red Irish Lord 162
Red Rockfish. 144
Red Salmon. 117
Red Sea Catfish 247
Redbanded Rockfish. 141
Redstripe Rockfish 141
Redtail Surfperch 124
Remora. 249
Ribbonfish. 246
Right Halibut. 103
Robalito 197
Robalo 196
Rock Bass 183
Rock Cod 135
Rock Greenling. 156
Rock Sole 105
Rockfish 183
Rockfish, Black. 133
Rockfish, Black-and-Yellow. 132
Rockfish, Blue. 134
Rockfish, Brown 135
Rockfish, Canary. 136
Rockfish, China. 137
Rockfish, Copper 137
Rockfish, Cow. 138
Rockfish, Grass. 138
Rockfish, Greenspotted 139
Rockfish, Kelp. 139
Rockfish, Olive 140
Rockfish, Quillback. 140
Rockfish, Redbanded 141
Rockfish, Redstripe. 141
Rockfish, Rosy 142
Rockfish, Silvergray. 142
Rockfish, Speckled 143
Rockfish, Tiger 143
Rockfish, Vermilion 144
Rockfish, Widow. 144
Rockfish, Yelloweye. 145
Rockfish, Yellowtail 145
Romeo Croaker 76
Roncador 91
Roosterfish. 58
Rosy Rockfish. 142
Rough Jacket. 107
Round Herring 261
Round Stingray 229
Roundhead Rockfish. 139
Roundnose Flounder 104
Rubberlip Seaperch 125
Runner, Rainbow. 57
Sailfish 34
Salema. 235
Salmon Grouper. 134
Salmon Shark 215
Salmon, Chinook 111
Salmon, Chum 112
Salmon, Coho 113

Salmon, Humpback. 116
Salmon, King. 111
Salmon, Pink 116
Salmon, Sockeye 117
Sand Bass, Goldspotted 171
Sand Bass, Spotted 181
Sand Eel 259
Sand Lance, Pacific 259
Sand Sole 106
Sanddab, Pacific. 98
Sardine, Pacific 260
Sargo. 236
Sargo, Carruco 234
Sargo, Spotted Head. 232
Saury, Pacific 260
Sawfish, Largetooth 229
Sawtail Grouper 178
Scad, Bigeye. 43
Scad, Mexican 51
Scalloped Hammerhead 216
Scalyfin Flounder 99
Scorpionfish, California. 135
Sculpin, Pacific Staghorn 161
Sea Bass 133
Sea Bass, Black 167
Sea Bass, Giant 167
Sea Catfish 247
Sea Chub 242
Seabass, Shortfin. 85
Seabass, White 92
Seaperch 128
Seaperch, Rubberlip 125
Seaperch, White 129
Shad 244
Shad, American. 254
Shad, Common. 254
Shad, Threadfin 263
Shark, Angel 202
Shark, Blacktip 203
Shark, Blue 204
Shark, Bonnethead 205
Shark, Bull. 206
Shark, Common Thresher 207
Shark, Dusky. 208
Shark, Galapagos. 209
Shark, Gray Smoothhound 209
Shark, Great White. 222
Shark, Hammerhead. 210
Shark, Lemon 211
Shark, Leopard 212
Shark, Mako 217
Shark, Nurse. 213
Shark, Oceanic Whitetip. 214
Shark, Pacific Sharpnose. 215
Shark, Salmon 215
Shark, Scalloped Hammerhead. 216
Shark, Silky 218
Shark, Smooth Hammerhead. 218
Shark, Soupfin. 219
Shark, Spinner. 203
Shark, Spiny Dogfish 220

Shark, Thresher. 207
Shark, Tiger. 221
Shark, White 222
Shark, Whitenose 223
Sharksucker 249
Sheepshead, California 64
Shiner Perch 126
Shortbill Spearfish 35
Shortfin Corvina. 85
Shortfin Mako. 217
Shovelnose Guitarfish. 228
Shovelnose Shark 205
Sierra 24
Sierra, Gulf 21
Silky Shark 218
Silver Mullet 250
Silver Perch 244
Silver Salmon 113
Silver Smelt. 262
Silver Surfperch 127
Silvergray Rockfish 142
Skate, Big. 226
Skate, California 227
Skipjack Tuna 25
Smelt, Longfin 258
Smelt, Rainbow. 261
Smelt, Surf. 262
Smelt, Whitebait 263
Smooth Hammerhead 218
Smooth Sculpin. 161
Snakefish. 243
Snapper, Amarillo 186
Snapper, Barred. 187
Snapper, Blue-and-Gold 188
Snapper, Colorado 189
Snapper, Jordan's 190
Snapper, Mullet 190
Snapper, Pacific Cubera 191
Snapper, Pacific Red 192
Snapper, Spotted Rose 193
Snapper, Yellow 186
Snook, Bigeye 198
Snook, Black 196
Snook, Humpback. 199
Snook, Little 197
Snook, Longspine 197
Snook, White 196
Snowy Grouper 179
Sockeye Salmon 117
Sole, Bigmouth 96
Sole, Butter. 99
Sole, C-O 100
Sole, Flathead 102
Sole, Petrale 104
Sole, Rock. 105
Sole, Sand 106
Soupfin Shark 219
Southern Bluefin Tuna 26
Southern Halibut 97
Spadefish, Pacific. 242
Spanish Jack 57

Spearfish, Shortbill 35
Speckled Grouper 182
Speckled Rockfish. 143
Spinner Shark 203
Spiny Dogfish 220
Spotfin Croaker 86
Spottail Grunt. 237
Spotted Cabrilla 180
Spotted Rose Snapper 193
Spotted Sand Bass 181
Spring Salmon. 111
Starry Flounder 107
Starry Grouper. 169
Starstudded Grouper. 182
Steelhead 117
Stingray, Round 229
Stolzmann's Corvina. 87
Striped Angelfish. 242
Striped Bass 183
Striped Bonito 27
Striped Corvina 88
Striped Jack. 47
Striped Marlin. 36
Striped Mullet. 250
Striped Surfperch 128
Striped Tuna 25
Striper. 183
Sturgeon, Green 67
Sturgeon, White 73
Sunapee 110
Surf Smelt 262
Surffish 78
Surfperch, Barred 120
Surfperch, Black 121
Surfperch, Calico 122
Surfperch, Rainbow 123
Surfperch, Redtail 124
Surfperch, Silver 127
Surfperch, Striped. 128
Surfperch, Walleye 129
Swordfish 37
Tarpon 71
Thread Herring 262
Threadfin Jack. 59
Threadfin Shad 263
Threadfin, Yellow. 251
Threadfish. 40
Tiger Grouper 177
Tiger Rockfish 143
Tiger Shark. 221
Tilefish 241
Tinker Mackerel 23
Tomcod, Pacific. 150
Tope Shark 219
Toro 251
Torpedo Ray 228
Totoaba. 89
Totuava 89
Trevally, Bigeye 42
Trevally, Bluefin 45
Trevally, Giant 60

Trevally, Golden 47
Triggerfish, Finescale. 245
Tripletail 72
Trout, Cutthroat. 114
Trout, Dolly Varden. 115
Trout, Kelp 154
Trout, Rainbow 117
Trout, Rock. 156
Trout, White 110
True Cod 148
Tuna, Bigeye 17
Tuna, Bluefin 26
Tuna, Skipjack 25
Tuna, Yellowfin. 29
Turbot, C-O 100
Turbot, Diamond 101
Turkey Red Rockfish 145
Turrum 60
Tyee 111
Ulua 60
Ulua, Yellow. 47
Union Snook 199
Vermilion Rockfish 144
Wahoo 28
Walleye Pollock 151
Walleye Surfperch 129
Wavyline Grunt 237
Whaler, Blue. 204
White Corvina. 90
White Croaker. 91
White Mullet 250
White Seabass 92
White Seaperch 129
White Shark. 222
White Snook 196
White Sturgeon 73
White Trout 110
Whitebait Smelt. 263
Whitebelly Rockfish. 137
Whitefish, Ocean 241
Whitenose Shark 223
Whitespotted Greenling 157
Whiting, California 78
Widow Rockfish. 144
Yellow Bobo 251
Yellow Irish Lord 163
Yellow Shark 211
Yellow Snapper. 186
Yellow Ulua. 47
Yellowbacked Rockfish. 137
Yelleye Rockfish. 145
Yellowfin Croaker 93
Yellowfin Tuna 29
Yellowstripe Rockfish. 137
Yellowtail 61
Yellowtail Rockfish 145
Zapatero. 50

Getting Pacific about It

It's fitting that author Vic Dunaway turns to the Pacific Ocean to write this fifth guidebook in his best-selling "Sport Fish" series.

In a sense, Vic returns to his roots in a land that actually caused the Pacific Ocean in the first place, albeit three million years earlier (see Introduction).

Author Dunaway spent many of his pre-spawning years in Panama, immersing his youthful and curious mind in fish and fishing, laying the groundwork for a career that would establish him as perhaps America's best all-around fishing writer.

Along the way, Vic picked up biological expertise that might make some professors blush, but it was more important to him that he learn the ways of fish from an angler's viewpoint.

His four previous Sport Fish books cover Florida, the Atlantic, Gulf of Mexico and North American freshwater species.

The Pacific book rounds out a library quintet that offers valuable down-to-earth, or down-to-water, information for anglers everywhere.

Colorful identification paintings of each species were meticulously done exclusively for this guide by artists Kevin Brant and Joe Suroviec, both of whom are excellent fishermen themselves.